Probeware Lab Manual

Prentice Hall
Physical Science

Concepts in Action
With Earth and Space Science

PEARSON

Prentice Hall

Boston, Massachusetts
Upper Saddle River, New Jersey

Probeware Lab Manual

Prentice Hall
Physical Science
Concepts in Action
With Earth and Space Science

ISBN 0-13-069976-4

5 6 7 8 9 10   10 09 08 07

Contents

Introduction   v
PASCO Hardware and Software   vi
Vernier Hardware and Software   ix
Texas Instruments Hardware and Software   xi
Laboratory Safety   xv
Laboratory Materials and Equipment Master Lists   xx

PASCO Lab
Textbook Correlation

1. Investigating Changes in Temperature   Exploration Lab, p. 92   2
   During Heating of Solids
2. Predicting the Density of an Element   Exploration Lab, p. 150   7
3. Preparing a Salt by Neutralization   Exploration Lab, p. 254   11
4. Investigating a Balloon Jet   Exploration Lab, p. 383   15
5. Determining Buoyant Force   Exploration Lab, p. 405   19
6. Investigating a Spring Clip   Application Lab, p. 467   23
7. Using Specific Heat to Analyze Metals   Design Your Own Lab, p. 493   27
8. Evaluating Electrical Safety   Forensics Lab, p. 623   31
9. Investigating an Electric Generator   Application Lab, p. 648   35
10. Determining Relative Humidity   Exploration Lab, p. 783   39

Vernier Lab
Textbook Correlation

1. Investigating Changes in Temperature   Exploration Lab, p. 92   44
   During Heating of Solids
2. Predicting the Density of an Element   Exploration Lab, p. 150   47
3. Preparing a Salt by Neutralization   Exploration Lab, p. 254   51
4. Investigating a Balloon Jet   Exploration Lab, p. 383   55
5. Determining Buoyant Force   Exploration Lab, p. 405   58
6. Investigating a Spring Clip   Application Lab, p. 467   61
7. Using Specific Heat to Analyze Metals   Design Your Own Lab, p. 493   64
8. Evaluating Electrical Safety   Forensics Lab, p. 623   67
9. Investigating an Electric Generator   Application Lab, p. 648   70
10. Determining Relative Humidity   Exploration Lab, p. 783   74

Texas Instruments Lab

		Textbook Correlation	
1.	Investigating Changes in Temperature During Heating of Solids	Exploration Lab, p. 92	80
2.	Predicting the Density of an Element	Exploration Lab, p. 150	83
3.	Preparing a Salt by Neutralization	Exploration Lab, p. 254	87
4.	Investigating a Balloon Jet	Exploration Lab, p. 383	91
5.	Determining Buoyant Force	Exploration Lab, p. 405	94
6.	Investigating a Spring Clip	Application Lab, p. 467	97
7.	Using Specific Heat to Analyze Metals	Design Your Own Lab, p. 493	100
8.	Evaluating Electrical Safety	Forensics Lab, p. 623	103
9.	Investigating an Electric Generator	Application Lab, p. 648	106
10.	Determining Relative Humidity	Exploration Lab, p. 783	110

Teacher Notes and Answers

PASCO Labs	114
Vernier and Texas Instruments Labs	123

Introduction

All of the labs in this manual have been adapted from selected labs in Prentice Hall's *Physical Science With Earth and Space Science* student edition, so you can be confident these labs will support your curriculum goals. Exploration labs allow students to practice and develop science methods. Students develop investigation skills and apply concepts in engaging real-world contexts while completing Forensics and Application Labs. During the Design Your Own Lab, students design and carry out an open-ended experiment.

The benefits of probeware labs should quickly become evident. Probeware sensors and user-friendly software simplify data collection in the classroom and in the field. As students become familiar with the probeware software and hardware, collecting, graphing, and analyzing data become almost effortless. By simplifying the data-gathering process, probeware lets students focus on drawing conclusions. Students then reap the rewards of a much fuller conceptual understanding.

Prentice Hall's *Physical Science With Earth and Space Science Probeware Lab Manual* is designed to meet your needs whether you are using Vernier, Texas Instruments, or PASCO® hardware and software. The CD-ROM in the front of this Lab Manual contains user guides, experiment files, and electronic labs to make it easier than ever to get started and enjoy productive lab experiences. When installed, many of the files from the CD-ROM will automatically set up a computer to use probeware sensors. This makes collecting data for most labs as easy as plugging in a sensor.

On the following pages you will find an introduction to each type of hardware and software. Additional information can be found in the user guides included on the CD-ROM and with your probeware equipment.

As always, safety must be the highest priority in the laboratory. Please make sure you and your students have reviewed the safety instructions and guidelines on pages xv–xix before working in the lab.

PASCO® Hardware and Software

PASCO has been providing innovative solutions for science educators worldwide since 1964. Introduced in 2000, the PASPORT® line of sensors allows students to harness the power of up-to-date computer technology to make electronic measurements. The DataStudio® software records, analyzes, and displays the data and runs on both Apple® Macintosh® and Microsoft® Windows® computers. With the Xplorer® handheld data logger and PASPORT sensors, students can make measurements away from the computer and then download data into the computer for further analysis.

The included CD-ROM contains DataStudio workbook files and pre-set configuration files that are designed for the *Probeware Lab Manual* that accompanies the new Prentice Hall *Physical Science With Earth and Space Science* textbook by Wysession, Frank, and Yancopoulos.

The workbook is a special display in the DataStudio program. A workbook file (**WB.ds) contains text, graphics, and data displays such as graphs and tables. A typical workbook file includes background information, materials, illustrated setup procedures, detailed instructions for recording data, and questions for analysis and conclusion.

A configuration file (**CF.ds) has appropriate data displays and analysis tools for the lab activity. Both the workbook file and the configuration file are interactive—when a student starts recording data, the workbook or configuration file displays the data in real time.

A workbook or configuration file combines the software (DataStudio) and hardware (PASPORT sensors) in a way that helps the student focus on the concept being studied rather than the technology being used.

Each DataStudio file is designed to integrate seamlessly into your unique classroom setting. The content, its structure, and underlying processes are carefully selected with regard to the *National Science Education Standards* and your Prentice Hall *Physical Science With Earth and Space Science* text.

Quick Start

Step 1. Install the DataStudio program. *Note:* DataStudio Lite can be installed by double-clicking on the Install DataStudio button on the enclosed CD-ROM. The complete DataStudio program is available online from PASCO at www.pasco.com.

Step 2. Install the DataStudio workbook and configuration files from the enclosed CD-ROM. *Note:* If the installer program does not automatically start when you click on Install PASCO Files, find the program file Setup (Macintosh) or Setup.exe (Windows) on the CD-ROM. Double-click on the file and follow the on-screen directions.

Step 3. Connect a USB link or the Xplorer data logger to a USB port on the computer. Plug the appropriate PASPORT sensor into the link or Xplorer. The PASPORTAL window will automatically open. (The window shows all the files that can use the sensor that is plugged in.)

Step 4. Select a workbook (**WB.ds) or configuration (**CF.ds) file from the list in the PASPORTAL window. Double-click on the file name or click on Open Selected Workbook. The DataStudio file opens automatically and you are ready to do science.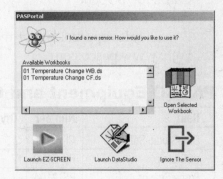

The Workbook file describes everything a student needs to successfully accomplish the lab activity.

If you use a Configuration file, follow the instructions included in the lab manual.

About Xplorer, PASCO's New Data Logger

The Xplorer is the new data logger from PASCO. Easy to use and versatile, the Xplorer is another educational tool in the PASPORT line of sensors and electronic measurement devices.

The Xplorer has plug-and-play capability—connect a PASPORT sensor and you're ready to start recording data! The battery-powered Xplorer can be used with all PASPORT sensors.

The Xplorer can be used as a data logger without a computer for stand-alone operation. Expand the logging flexibility back in the classroom by plugging the Xplorer into the USB port of your PC or Macintosh. Extend your teaching and learning environment using DataStudio, PASCO's powerful data collection and analysis software.

Prentice Hall and PASCO

This collaborative project between Prentice Hall and PASCO represents the next generation of science curriculum materials. Our strategy builds upon the prior successes of each company. The result is a set of technological activities that bring ambitious and meaningful science teaching and learning into your unique classroom.

Contact Information

Contact PASCO for more information about PASPORT, DataStudio, the Xplorer data logger, and the other science equipment designed and manufactured by PASCO.

Write:

PASCO
10101 Foothills Blvd.
Roseville, California 95747-7100
Call: 800-772-8700 toll-free in the United States
Call: 916-786-3800
Fax: 916-786-8905
E-mail: sales@pasco.com *or* techsupp@pasco.com
Web: www.pasco.com

PASCO Equipment and Ordering Information

Item	Number	Qty	Lab
DataStudio Software	CI-6781	1	All
USB Link	PS-2100	2	All except 2
Force Sensor	PS-2104	1	5, 6
Humidity Sensor	PS-2124	1	10
Motion Sensor	PS-2103	1	4
pH Sensor	PS-2102	1	3
Temperature Sensor	PS-2125	1	1, 7, 10
Voltage-Current Sensor	PS-2115	1	8, 9
Base and Support Rod	ME-9355	1	4, 7
Buret Clamp	SE-9446	1	7
Ohaus Balance	SE-8758	1	2, 7
Xplorer *	PS-2000	1	All (optional)
PowerLink **	PS-2001	1	All (optional)

* The PASPORT Xplorer (PS-2000) is a battery-powered handheld data logger that can be used to record data without being connected to a computer.

**The PASPORT PowerLink (PS-2001) supports up to three PASPORT Sensors. The PowerLink can be powered by two "C" cells so it can record data remotely when connected to a portable computer or a Palm™ handheld PDA.

Vernier Hardware and Software

Since 1981 Vernier Software & Technology has been a leader in the development of data collection tools and software for science and math educators. Data collection products are available for Macintosh computers, PC computers, Texas Instruments graphing calculators and Palm™ handhelds. Vernier's products are highly regarded for their ease of use, reliability, and affordability. Vernier has developed more than 40 sensors that simplify data collection in the classroom or in the field, and make it possible to gather measurements that were difficult or impossible to make in the past. Auto-ID sensors and user-friendly software simplify data collection and analysis. A generous site license policy and reasonably priced sensors make data collection technology affordable. All Vernier products carry a five-year limited warranty against defects in materials and workmanship.

For customer support, product information, and current prices, please contact

Vernier Software & Technology
13979 SW Millikan Way
Beaverton, Oregon 97005-2886

Phone: (888) 837-6437
Fax: (503) 277-2440

Web site: www.vernier.com
E-mail: info@vernier.com

Ordering Information

Item	Order Code	Price
LabPro interface	LABPRO	$220
Logger Pro 3 Software	LP	$99
Motion Detector	MD-BTD	$64
Dual-Range Force Sensor	DFS-BTA	$99
pH Sensor	PH-BTA	$74
(2 each) Stainless-Steel Temperature Probe	TMP-BTA	$29
Current Probe	DCP-BTA	$37

Logger *Pro* 3 Quick Start

Before using the labs in this manual, you must install the Logger *Pro* 3 experiment files by following the instructions on the attached CD-ROM. The CD-ROM provides only the experiment files; Logger *Pro* 3 software is sold separately by Vernier. After the experiment files and Logger *Pro* 3 software are installed, follow these steps.

Attach interface and sensor

- Attach a LabPro to the computer using the supplied cable. On the Macintosh you can use any serial port, including the modem and printer ports, or a USB port. On the PC you can use any of the COM1, 2, 3 or 4 serial ports, or the USB port.
- Attach the power adapter to the interface and to a source of house current.
- Attach a sensor to the interface.

Start up Logger *Pro*

- Locate the Logger *Pro* 3 icon and double-click on it, or use the Start menu (Windows 95/98/NT/2000/XP).

Logger Pro 3.1

Configure Logger *Pro* 3 for your experiment

- Choose Open from the File menu, and choose an experiment file from the folder containing the experiment files. Sensor calibration and data collection parameters are automatically loaded with the experiment file.

Collect data

- At the appropriate time in your experiment, click on [▶Collect]. Logger *Pro* should begin collecting data, and if a graph is present, plotting data on the screen.

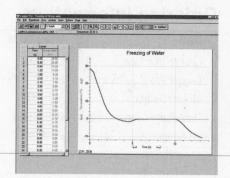

Adjust graph

- You can adjust most features of the graph by double clicking on the graph and making changes in the resulting dialog box.

If you need more information for using Logger *Pro* 3, refer to the extensive online help.

Texas Instruments Hardware and Software

Let your students discover how math and science affect the world around them by developing hypotheses, completing experiments, and forming conclusions. The CBL 2™ provides the easiest, most accessible way for students to collect and analyze real-world data!

- CBL 2 is easy to use.
- Some products take a lot of time and effort to set up and use—not so with the CBL 2.
- CBL 2 has sturdy construction for classroom use.
- Built-in software (DataMate) is transferred to your calculator with the push of a single button. Start collecting data right away, or quickly set up the CBL 2 for more sophisticated applications.

Collect data with one of more than 40 sensors from Vernier Software & Technology. The range of sensors available with CBL 2 allows you and your students to perform a wide range of investigations. More detailed information about the CBL 2 is available in the user's guide found on the CD in the Lab Manual. Just launch the CD-ROM and click on Texas Instruments. There is also updated information at the TI Web site.

General Information

Contact the TI Customer Support Line to order products, before returning a product for service, or if you have general questions about using a product.

Call: 800-TI-CARES (800-842-2737)

Monday–Thursday   8:00 A.M.–7:00 P.M. CST

Friday   10:00 A.M.–7:00 P.M. CST

E-mail: ti-cares@ti.com

Write: Texas Instruments
Customer Support Line
PO Box 650311, MS3962
Dallas, Texas 75265

Technical Assistance

The TI Technical Assistance Group is trained to answer your technical questions about TI calculators, software, and accessories.

Call: 972-917-8324 (This is not a toll-free number.)

Monday–Thursday   8:00 A.M.–7:00 P.M. CST

Friday   10:00 A.M.–7:00 P.M. CST

Email: ti-cares@ti.com

Write: Texas Instruments
Technical Assistance Group
PO Box 650311, MS3962
Dallas, Texas 75265

Ordering Information

All items can be ordered from Vernier. Visit their Web site at www.vernier.com.

Item	Order Code	Price
CBL 2 interface including one Stainless-Steel Temperature Probe and Voltage Probe	CBL2	$166
Motion Detector	MD-BTD	$64
Dual-Range Force Sensor	DFS-BTA	$99
pH Sensor	PH-BTA	$74
(2 each) Stainless-Steel Temperature Probe	TMP-BTA	$29
Current Probe	DCP-BTA	$37

Texas Instruments Startup

Vernier's DataMate program for the TI graphing calculators is used to collect, examine, analyze and graph data. It is a powerful yet easy-to-use program. Use the link cable to connect the CBL 2 or LabPro to the TI graphing calculator. Firmly press in the link cables. Use the following steps to start the DataMate program on your calculator:

TI-73, TI-82, and TI-83 Calculators

Press PRGM and then press the calculator key for the number that precedes DATAMATE (usually 1). Press ENTER. An introductory screen will appear, followed by the main screen.

TI-83 Plus and TI-83 Plus Silver Edition Calculators

Press APPS and then press the calculator key for the number that precedes DATAMATE. Press ENTER. An introductory screen will appear, followed by the main screen.

TI-86 Calculators

Press PRGM, press F1 to select NAMES, and press the menu key that represents DataMate. (DATAM is usually F1). Press ENTER and wait for the main screen to load.

TI-89, TI-92, TI-92 Plus, and Voyage 200 Calculators

Press 2nd VAR-LINK. Use the cursor pad to scroll down to DATAMATE and then press ENTER. Press) to complete the open parenthesis of DATAMATE(on the entry line. Press ENTER. An introductory screen will appear, followed by the main screen.

For more details on the program features, refer to the manuals that accompany the CBL 2 and LabPro. You can also download the *DataMate Guidebook* from the Vernier Web site (www.vernier.com).

Non-Auto ID Sensor Setup

1. Set up the calculator and interface for the sensor being used (for example, temperature probe).
   a. Select SETUP from the main screen.
   b. If the calculator displays a probe name in CH 1, the sensor has an auto-ID. Proceed directly to Step 2. If there is no name displayed, continue on to 1c to set up your sensor manually.
   c. Press ⌐ENTER⌐ to select CH 1.
   d. Select the sensor type (for example, TEMPERATURE or PH) from the SELECT SENSOR menu.
   e. Select the exact name of the sensor you are using (for example, DIR CONNECT TEMP (C) or DIR CONNECT TEMP (F)) from the sensor-type menu (for example, TEMPERATURE).
2. Set up the data-collection mode.
   a. To select MODE, press ⌐▲⌐ once and press ⌐ENTER⌐ .
   b. Select a data collection mode (for example, TIME GRAPH or EVENTS WITH ENTRY) from the SELECT MODE menu.
   c. If you selected LOG DATA, EVENTS WITH ENTRY, SINGLE POINT, SELECTED EVENTS, or RETURN TO SET-UP SCREEN, proceed directly to step 2g. If you selected TIME GRAPH, the TIME GRAPH SETTINGS menu appears. To change the default settings, select CHANGE TIME SETTINGS.
   d. Key in the time between samples in seconds
   e. Key in the number of samples and press ⌐ENTER⌐ .
   f. Select OK to return to the setup screen.
   g. Select OK again to return to the main screen.

Transferring a Calculator Graph to a Computer for Printing

Many labs in this manual have an option to print a graph. To print a graph you will need a TI-GRAPH LINK™ cable and either TI Connect™ or TI-GRAPH LINK software. Before doing a lab that requires printing, you may want to show your students how to print graphs.

Using TI Connect to capture a screen with a Windows computer

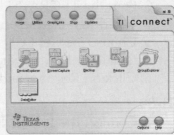

Start the TI Connect software. The main TI Connect screen will appear.

1. Be sure the device is connected to your computer and is turned on.
2. On your device, display the screen you want to capture.
3. On the TI Connect™ home screen, click on the ScreenCapture icon. The program will capture the screen and display it on your computer.
4. You can now print the screen, paste it into another document, or save the screen to a file.

Using TI Connect to capture a screen
with a Macintosh computer

1. Be sure the device is connected to your computer and is turned on.
2. On the menu bar, select Connection and then select your device type.
3. Select the port to which the device is attached and click on Connect. If the connection is successful, a calculator window will appear. If any errors occur, follow the on-screen instructions.
4. Select the calculator window and then select Get Screen from the Window menu.
5. You can now print the screen, paste it into another document, or save the screen to a file.

Using TI-GRAPH LINK with a Windows computer
and TI-82, TI-85 or TI-86

If you are using a TI-82, TI-85, or TI-86 and a Windows computer, you will need to use the TI-GRAPH LINK program to print graphs.

TI-82

1. Connect the TI-GRAPH LINK cable to the serial port of your computer and to the port at the bottom edge of the TI-82.
2. The graph that you want to print should be displayed on the calculator screen.
3. Start the TI-GRAPH LINK (82) software on your computer.
4. Pull down the Link menu.
5. Choose the Get LCD from TI-82 option. Choose the Printer (small) or Printer (large) option.
6. Click on Receive, and then click on OK.

TI-85

1. Connect the TI-GRAPH LINK cable to the serial port of your computer and to the port at the bottom edge of the TI-85.
2. The graph that you want to print should be displayed on the calculator screen.
3. Start the TI-GRAPH LINK (85) software on your computer.
4. Pull down the Link menu.
5. Choose the Get LCD from TI-85 option. Choose the Printer (small) or Printer (large) option.
6. Click on Receive, and then click on OK.

TI-86

1. Connect the TI-GRAPH LINK cable to the serial port of your computer and to the port at the bottom edge of the TI-86.
2. The graph that you want to print should be displayed on the calculator screen.
3. Start the TI-GRAPH LINK (86) software on your computer.
4. Pull down the Link menu and choose the Get Screen.
5. Click on the Get Screen button.
6. Click on the Print button.

Laboratory Safety

Safety Symbols

These symbols appear in laboratory activities. They alert you to possible dangers and remind you to work carefully.

General Safety Awareness Read all directions for an experiment several times. Follow the directions exactly as they are written. If you are in doubt, ask your teacher for assistance.

Physical Safety If the lab includes physical activity, use caution to avoid injuring yourself or others. Tell your teacher if there is a reason that you should not participate.

Safety Goggles Always wear safety goggles to protect your eyes in any activity involving chemicals, heating, or the possibility of broken glassware.

Lab Apron Wear a laboratory apron to protect your skin and clothing from harmful chemicals or hot materials.

Plastic Gloves Wear disposable plastic gloves to protect yourself from contact with chemicals that can be harmful. Keep your hands away from your face. Dispose of gloves according to your teacher's instructions.

Heating Use a clamp or tongs to hold hot objects. Test an object by first holding the back of your hand near it. If you feel heat, the object may be too hot to handle.

Heat-Resistant Gloves Hot plates, hot water, and hot glassware can cause burns. Never touch hot objects with your bare hands. Use an oven mitt or other hand protection.

Flames Tie back long hair and loose clothing, and put on safety goggles before using a burner. Follow instructions from your teacher for lighting and extinguishing burners.

No Flames If flammable materials are present, make sure there are no flames, sparks, or exposed sources of heat.

Electric Shock To avoid an electric shock, never use electrical equipment near water, or when the equipment or your hands are wet. Use only sockets that accept a three-prong plug. Be sure cords are untangled and cannot trip anyone. Disconnect equipment that is not in use.

Fragile Glassware Handle fragile glassware, such as thermometers, test tubes, and beakers, with care. Do not touch broken glass. Notify your teacher if glassware breaks. Never use chipped or cracked glassware.

Corrosive Chemical Avoid getting corrosive chemicals on your skin or clothing, or in your eyes. Do not inhale the vapors. Wash your hands after completing the activity.

Poison Do not let any poisonous chemical get on your skin, and do not inhale its vapor. Wash your hands after completing the activity.

Fumes When working with poisonous or irritating vapors, work in a well-ventilated area. Never test for an odor unless instructed to do so by your teacher. Avoid inhaling a vapor directly. Use a wafting motion to direct vapor toward your nose.

Sharp Object Use sharp instruments only as directed. Scissors, scalpels, pins, and knives are sharp and can cut or puncture your skin. Always direct sharp edges and points away from yourself and others.

Disposal All chemicals and other materials used in the laboratory must be disposed of safely. Follow your teacher's instructions.

Hand Washing Before leaving the lab, wash your hands thoroughly with soap or detergent, and warm water. Lather both sides of your hands and between your fingers. Rinse well.

Science Safety

Laboratory work can be exciting, but it can be dangerous if you don't follow safety rules. Ask your teacher to explain any rules you don't understand. Always pay attention to safety symbols and **CAUTION** statements.

General Safety Rules and First Aid

1. Read all directions for an experiment several times. Follow the directions exactly as they are written. If you are in doubt, ask your teacher for assistance.
2. Never perform unauthorized or unsupervised labs, or handle equipment without specific permission.
3. When you design an experiment, do not start until your teacher has approved your plan.
4. If a lab includes physical activity, use caution to avoid injuring yourself or others. Tell your teacher if there is a reason that you should not participate.
5. Never eat, drink, or bring food into the laboratory.
6. Report all accidents to your teacher immediately.
7. Learn the correct ways to deal with a burn, a cut, and acid splashed in your eyes or on your skin.
8. Be aware of the location of the first-aid kit. Your teacher should administer any required first aid.
9. Report any fire to your teacher immediately. Find out the location of the fire extinguisher, the fire alarm, and the phone where emergency numbers are listed.

Dress Code

10. Always wear safety goggles to protect your eyes when working in the lab. Avoid wearing contact lenses. If you must wear contact lenses, ask your teacher what precautions you should take.
11. Wear a laboratory apron to protect your skin and clothing from harmful chemicals or hot materials.
12. Wear disposable plastic gloves to protect yourself from contact with chemicals that can be harmful. Keep your hands away from your face. Dispose of gloves according to your teacher's instructions.
13. Tie back long hair and loose clothing. Remove any jewelry that could contact chemicals or flames.

Heating and Fire Safety

14. Hot plates, hot water, and hot glassware can cause burns. Never touch hot objects with your bare hands. Use an oven mitt or other hand protection.

15. Use a clamp or tongs to hold hot objects. Test an object by first holding the back of your hand near it. If you feel heat on the back of your hand, the object may be too hot to handle.
16. Tie back long hair and loose clothing, and put on safety goggles before using a burner. Follow instructions from your teacher for lighting and extinguishing burners. If the flame leaps out of a burner as you are lighting it, turn the gas off. Never leave a flame unattended or reach across a flame. Make sure your work area is not cluttered with materials.
17. If flammable materials are present, make sure there are no flames, sparks, or exposed sources of heat.
18. Never heat a chemical without your teacher's permission. Chemicals that are harmless when cool can be dangerous when heated. When heating a test tube, point the opening away from you and others in case the contents splash or boil out of the test tube.
19. Never heat a closed container. Expanding hot gases may cause the container to explode.

Using Electricity Safely

20. To avoid an electric shock, never use electrical equipment near water, or when the equipment or your hands are wet. Use ground fault circuit interrupter (GFCI) outlets if you or your equipment may come into contact with moisture.
21. Use only sockets that accept a three-prong plug. Never use two-prong extension cords or adapters. When removing an electrical plug from a socket or extension cord, grasp the plug, not the cord.
22. Disconnect equipment that is not in use. Be sure cords are untangled and cannot trip anyone.
23. Do not use damaged electrical equipment. Look for dangerous conditions such as bare wires or frayed cords. Report damaged equipment immediately.

Using Glassware Safely

24. Handle fragile glassware, such as thermometers, test tubes, and beakers, with care. Do not touch broken glass. Notify your teacher if glassware breaks. Never use chipped or cracked glassware.
25. Never force glass tubing into a stopper. Your teacher will demonstrate the proper methods.
26. Never heat glassware that is not thoroughly dry. Use a wire screen to protect glassware from flames.
27. Hot glassware may not appear hot. Never pick up glassware without first checking to see if it is hot.
28. Never eat or drink from laboratory glassware.

Using Chemicals Safely

29. Do not let any corrosive or poisonous chemicals get on your skin or clothing, or in your eyes. When working with poisonous or irritating vapors, work in a well-ventilated area and wash your hands thoroughly after completing the activity.
30. Never test for an odor unless instructed by your teacher. Avoid inhaling a vapor directly. Use a wafting motion to direct vapor toward your nose.
31. Never mix chemicals "for the fun of it." You might produce a dangerous, possibly explosive substance.
32. Never touch, taste, or smell a chemical that you do not know for certain to be harmless.
33. Use only those chemicals listed in an investigation. Keep the lids on the containers when chemicals are not being used. To avoid contamination, never return chemicals to their original containers.
34. Take extreme care not to spill any chemicals. If a spill occurs, immediately ask your teacher about the proper cleanup procedure. Dispose of all chemicals as instructed by your teacher.
35. Be careful when working with acids or bases. Pour these chemicals over the sink, not over your workbench. If an acid or base gets on your skin or clothing, rinse it off with plenty of cold water. Immediately notify your teacher about an acid or base spill.
36. When diluting an acid, pour the acid into water. Never pour water into the acid.

Using Sharp Instruments

37. Use sharp instruments only as directed. Scissors, scalpels, pins, and knives are sharp and can cut or puncture your skin. Always direct sharp edges and points away from yourself and others.
38. Notify your teacher immediately if you cut yourself when in the laboratory.

End-of-Experiment Rules

39. All chemicals and any other materials used in the laboratory must be disposed of safely. Follow your teacher's instructions.
40. Clean up your work area and return all equipment to its proper place. Thoroughly clean glassware before putting it away.
41. Wash your hands thoroughly with soap, or detergent, and warm water. Lather both sides of your hands and between your fingers. Rinse well.
42. Check that all burners are off and the gas supply for the burners is turned off.

Emergency Procedures

Report any injury, accident, or spill to your teacher immediately.
Know the location of the closest eyewash fountain, fire blanket,
fire extinguisher, and shower.

SITUATION	SAFE RESPONSE
Burns	Immediately flush with cold water until the burning sensation subsides.
Fainting	Provide fresh air (for instance, open a window). Move the person so that the head is lower than the rest of the body. If breathing stops, use CPR.
Fire	Turn off all gas outlets. Unplug all appliances. Use a fire blanket or fire extinguisher to smother the fire. **CAUTION** *Do not cut off a person's air supply.*
Eye injury	Immediately flush the eye with running water. Remove contact lenses. Do not allow eye to be rubbed if a foreign object is present in the eye.
Minor cuts	Allow to bleed briefly. Wash with soap and water.
Poisoning	Note what substance was responsible. Alert teacher immediately.
Spills on skin	Flush with water.
Electric shock	Provide fresh air. Adjust the person's position so that the head is lower than the rest of the body.

Master Laboratory Materials and Equipment List

PASCO

Item	Quantity Per Group	Laboratory Number
Ohaus balance with serial port	1	2
PASPORT force sensor	1	5, 6
PASPORT humidity sensor (optional)	2	10
PASPORT motion sensor	1	4
PASPORT pH sensor	1	3
PASPORT temperature sensor	1	1, 7
PASPORT temperature sensor	2	10
PASPORT USB link or Xplorer	1	1, 3, 4, 5, 6, 7, 8, 9
PASPORT USB link	2	10
PASPORT voltage and current sensor	1	8, 9
Patch cords and alligator clips (supplied with voltage and current sensor)	1 set	9
Serial or USB cable	1	2
Data Studio Software	1	all

Vernier

Item	Quantity Per Group	Laboratory Number
LabPro interface	1	all
Logger *Pro* software	1	all
Vernier current Probe	1	9
Vernier dual-range force sensor	1	2, 5, 6
Vernier motion detector	1	4
Vernier pH sensor	1	3
Vernier stainless steel temperature probe	1	1, 7
Vernier stainless steel temperature probe	2	10
Vernier voltage probe	1	8

Texas Instruments

Item	Quantity Per Group	Laboratory Number
DataMate program	1	all
LabPro or CBL 2 interface	1	all
TI Graphing Calculator	1	all
Vernier current Probe	1	9
Vernier dual-range force sensor	1	2, 5, 6
Vernier motion detector	1	4
Vernier pH sensor	1	3
Vernier stainless steel temperature probe	1	1, 7
Vernier stainless steel temperature probe	2	10
Vernier voltage probe	1	8

Consumables

Item	Quantity Per Group	Laboratory Number
absorbent wick (gauze or flat shoe lace)	1	10
can	1	5
cardboard rectangle (about 6 cm × 20 cm)	1	4
crushed ice	1	1
disposable pipet	1	4
distilled water	10 mL	3
drinking straw	2	4
fishing line, 3-m length	2	4
graph paper	1 sheet	1, 2, 6, 9
heavy twine	1 roll	6
hydrochloric acid	8 mL	3
ice water	200 mL	7
labels	3	3
long balloon	4	4
masking tape	1 roll	4, 9, 10
paper towels	1 roll	5
phenolphthalein solution	8 mL	3
piece of shoelace, 5 cm long	1	10
sodium hydroxide solution	8 mL	3
string, 3-m length	1	4, 5
string, 50-cm length	1	7
test tube of lauric acid	1	1
unlined white paper	1	2

Nonconsumables

Item	Quantity Per Group	Laboratory Number
alligator clip	3	8
aluminum nail	several	7
balance	1	7
bar magnet	1	9
battery clip	1	8
battery, 9-volt	1	8
beaker, 100-mL	1	3
beaker, 25-mL	2	3
boiling water bath	1	7
cardboard rectangle	1	10
cardboard tube	1	9
C-clamp	1	6
chair	2	4
clamp	1	7
clock with second hand	1	1
crushed can	1	7
dropper pipet	3	3

Nonconsumables (*continued*)

Item	Quantity Per Group	Laboratory Number
foam cup with lid	1	7
forceps	1	2
glass stirring rod	1	1
graduated cylinder, 10-mL	1	3
graduated cylinder, 250-mL	1	5
graduated cylinder, 500-mL	1	7
graduated cylinder, 50-mL	1	2
hot plate	1	1, 3
insulated wire, 5-m length	1	9
large watch glass	1	3
lead shot	varies	2
meter stick	1	4
metric ruler	1	2, 6, 9
notepad or soft-cover book	1	9
periodic table	1	2
plastic tub	1	5
resistor, 1000-ohm	1	8
resistor, 100-ohm	1	8
resistor, 10-ohm	1	8
resistor, 1-ohm	1	8
ring stand	1	7
rock	1	5
scissors	1	2
silicon	varies	2
sponge	1	5
spring clip	1	6
standard mass, 100-g	1	5
steel bolt	10	7
stirring rod	3	3
support stand	1	4
test tube rack	1	3
test tube, 10-mL	2	3
threaded nut	2	4
tin	varies	2
wooden block tied to a fishing weight	1	5
yogurt cup with string	1	2

Safety Equipment

Item	Quantity Per Group	Laboratory Number
apron	several	1, 2, 3, 5, 7, 8, 10
goggles	several	all
plastic gloves	several	1, 2, 3, 10

Contents

PASCO Lab

Textbook Correlation

1. Investigating Changes in Temperature During Heating of Solids — Exploration Lab, p. 92 — 2
2. Predicting the Density of an Element — Exploration Lab, p. 150 — 7
3. Preparing a Salt by Neutralization — Exploration Lab, p. 254 — 11
4. Investigating a Balloon Jet — Exploration Lab, p. 383 — 15
5. Determining Buoyant Force — Exploration Lab, p. 405 — 19
6. Investigating a Spring Clip — Application Lab, p. 467 — 23
7. Using Specific Heat to Analyze Metals — Design Your Own Lab, p. 493 — 27
8. Evaluating Electrical Safety — Forensics Lab, p. 623 — 31
9. Investigating an Electric Generator — Application Lab, p. 648 — 35
10. Determining Relative Humidity — Exploration Lab, p. 783 — 39

Teacher Notes and Answers

PASCO Labs — 114

Exploration Lab

Investigating Changes in Temperature During Heating of Solids

Lauric acid is a solid that is found in coconuts and processed foods that are made with coconut oil. Lauric acid is also used to make some soaps and cosmetics. In this lab, you will measure the temperature of ice and of lauric acid as these solids are heated and melt. You will graph the data you collect and compare the heating curves for ice and for lauric acid.

Problem

What happens to the temperature of a substance during a phase change?

Materials

- PASPORT USB link or Xplorer
- PASPORT temperature sensor
- 500-mL beaker
- crushed ice
- hot plate
- test tube of lauric acid
- glass stirring rod
- graph paper

Skills

Measuring, Using Graphs

Procedure 🌀 🔒 🖐 🔆 🧍

Part A: Heating Ice

1. Plug the USB link into the computer's USB port or use the Xplorer.
2. Plug the temperature sensor into the USB link or the Xplorer.

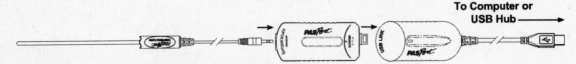

To Computer or USB Hub ➞

This will automatically launch the PASPortal window if you are connected to the computer.

3. Choose the appropriate electronic workbook or DataStudio configuration file from the PASPortal window.

- If you are using the PASCO electronic workbook specifically designed for this activity, then simply click on the workbook entitled

    01 Temperature Changes WB.ds

    Click on the Open Selected Workbook icon in the PASPortal window and go!

- If you are not using an electronic workbook, then click on the file entitled

    01 Temperature Changes CF.ds

    Click on the Open Selected Workbook icon in the PASPortal window and proceed with the following instructions.

4. Use the data table found on page 6 to record your data. You may need to add more rows to the end of your data table if the solids do not melt within 20 minutes.

5. Fill a 500-mL beaker halfway with crushed ice. **CAUTION** *Use care when handling glassware to avoid breakage. Wipe up any spilled ice right away to avoid slips and falls.*

6. Place the beaker on a hot plate. Don't turn the hot plate on yet. Insert the temperature sensor into the ice. Because it takes several seconds for the sensor to adjust to the temperature of its surroundings, wait 20 seconds. If you are connected to the computer, select Monitor Data from the Experiment menu on the DataStudio menu bar to begin collecting data. The temperature of the ice will appear in the digits display. Record this temperature next to the 0 minutes entry in your data table.

Select Monitor Data from the Experiment Menu

7. Click on ■ Stop to end data monitoring in the DataStudio window.

8. Turn the hot plate to a low setting. If you are collecting data using the DataStudio window, click on ▶ Start on the toolbar to begin. **CAUTION** *Be careful not to touch the hot plate because it could burn you.*

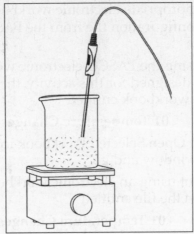

9. Observe and record the temperature at one-minute intervals until all the ice has changed to liquid water. Note the temperature at which you first observe liquid water and the temperature at which all the ice has changed to liquid water.

10. After all the ice has melted, make temperature measurements at one-minute intervals for five more minutes. Click on ■ Stop to end data collection. Turn off the hot plate.

11. Graph the data on your paper with time on the horizontal axis and temperature on the vertical axis. Label the point at which you first observed liquid water and the point at which all the ice had changed to liquid water.

Part B: Heating Lauric Acid

12. Empty the water from the beaker into the sink. Fill the beaker halfway with cool tap water.

13. Place a test tube containing lauric acid and the temperature sensor into the beaker. If necessary, add or remove water from the beaker so that the surface of the water is above the surface of the lauric acid but below the opening of the test tube.

14. Place the beaker on the hot plate and wait 20 seconds. If you are connected to the computer, select Monitor Data from the Experiment menu on the DataStudio menu bar to begin collecting data. The temperature of the lauric acid will appear in the digits display. Record this temperature next to the 0 minutes entry in your data table.

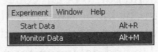

Select Monitor Data from the Experiment Menu

15. Repeat Steps 8 through 11 using the lauric acid instead of the ice. To keep the temperature the same throughout the water bath, use the stirring rod to stir the water. **CAUTION** *Remove the temperature sensor from the lauric acid while the lauric acid is still melted.*

Analyze and Conclude

1. Using Graphs Describe the shape of your graph for ice.

_____

_____

2. Analyzing Data What happened to the temperature of the ice-water mixture during the phase change?

_____

_____

_____

3. Comparing and Contrasting Compare the shapes of the graphs for ice and for lauric acid. Compare the melting points of ice and lauric acid.

_____

_____

_____

_____

Data Table

Time (minutes)	Temperature of Water (°C)	Temperature of Lauric Acid (°C)
0		
1		
2		
3		
4		
5		
6		
7		
8		
9		
10		
11		
12		
13		
14		
15		
16		
17		
18		
19		
20		

Exploration Lab

Predicting the Density of an Element

Density is a useful property for identifying and classifying elements. In this lab, you will determine the densities of three elements in Group 4A—silicon, tin, and lead. Then you will use your data to predict the density of another element in Group 4A—germanium.

Problem

Can the densities of elements within a group be used to accurately predict the density of another element in the group?

Materials

- Ohaus balance with serial port
- serial or USB cable
- unlined white paper
- scissors
- metric ruler
- forceps
- silicon
- tin
- lead shot
- 50-mL graduated cylinder
- graph paper
- periodic table

Skills

Measuring, Observing, Using Graphs, Calculating

Procedure 🐢 🎒 🔋 ✋ ✂️

Part A: Measuring Mass

1. Plug one end of the serial or USB cable into a serial or USB port on the computer.

2. Plug the other end of the cable into the appropriate port on the balance.

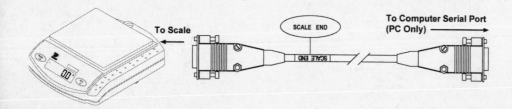

3. Start DataStudio and open the appropriate electronic workbook or DataStudio configuration file.

- If you are using the PASCO electronic workbook specifically designed for this activity, open the workbook entitled

02 Density of an Element WB.ds

and go!

- If you are not using an electronic workbook, then open the file entitled

02 Density of an Element CF.ds

and proceed with the following instructions.

4. Cut out three 10-cm × 10-cm pieces of paper from a sheet of unlined white paper. Label one piece of paper Silicon, the second Tin, and the third Lead. Find the mass of each piece of paper and record it in the data table at the end of the lab.

5. Using forceps, place the silicon onto the paper labeled Silicon. Find the mass of the silicon and the paper. Record this mass in your data table. Then, subtract the mass of the paper from the mass of the silicon and paper. Record the mass of silicon in your data table. Set the paper containing the silicon aside for now.

6. Repeat Step 5 to find the masses of tin and lead. (*Tip:* To prevent the lead shot from rolling off the paper, fold the edges of the paper up to form a shallow box.)

Part B: Measuring Volume

7. Place 25 mL of water in the graduated cylinder. Measure the volume of the water to the nearest 0.1 mL. Record the volume (in cm^3) in the data table at the end of the lab. (*Hint:* 1 mL = 1 cm^3)

8. Tilt the graduated cylinder and carefully pour the silicon from the paper into the graduated cylinder. Make sure that the silicon is completely covered by the water. Measure and record the volume of the water and silicon in your data table. Then, subtract the volume of water from the volume of the water and silicon. Record the result in your data table.

9. Repeat Steps 7 and 8 to find the volumes of tin and lead.

Part C: Calculating Density

10. To calculate the density of silicon, divide its mass by its volume.

$$\text{Density} = \frac{\text{Mass}}{\text{Volume}}$$

Record the density of silicon in your data table.

11. Repeat Step 10 to find the densities of tin and lead.

12. Make a line graph that shows the relationship between the densities of silicon, tin, and lead and the periods in which they are located in the periodic table. Place the number of the period (from 1 to 7) on the horizontal axis and the density (in g/cm^3) on the vertical axis. Draw a straight line that comes as close as possible to all three points.

13. Germanium is in Period 4. To estimate the density of germanium, draw a dotted vertical line from the 4 on the horizontal axis to the solid line. Then, draw a dotted horizontal line from the solid line to the vertical axis. Read and record the density of germanium.

14. Wash your hands with warm water and soap before you leave the laboratory.

Data Table

Element	Mass of Paper (g)	Mass of Paper and Element (g)	Mass of Element (g)	Volume of Water (cm³)	Volume of Water and Element (cm³)	Volume of Element (cm³)	Density of Element (g/cm³)
Silicon							
Tin							
Lead							

Analyze and Conclude

1. Classifying List lead, silicon, and tin in order of increasing density.

_____

_____

2. Comparing and Contrasting How does your estimate of the density of germanium compare with the actual density of germanium, which is 5.3 g/cm³?

_____

_____

3. Calculating Use the formula for percent error (PE) to calculate a percent error for your estimate of the density of germanium.

$$PE = \frac{\text{Estimated value} - \text{Accepted value}}{\text{Accepted value}} * 100$$

4. Drawing Conclusions How does the density of the elements change from silicon to lead in Group 4A?

_____

_____

Go Further

Use reference books or sites on the Internet to research properties of Group 4A elements. Construct a graph that shows how another property, such as melting point or boiling point, varies among the Group 4A elements you explored. Determine whether knowing the values for three of the elements would allow you to accurately predict a value for the fourth element.

Exploration Lab

Preparing a Salt by Neutralization

In this lab, you will prepare table salt by reacting hydrochloric acid (HCl) with sodium hydroxide (NaOH). To be sure that all of the acid and base have reacted, you will use phenolphthalein. You will first have to test the colors of this indicator with a known acid and base. After the acid and base have reacted, you will measure the pH of the solution with a pH sensor. Finally, you will evaporate the water and collect the sodium chloride.

Problem

How can you produce a salt by neutralization?

Materials

- PASPORT USB link or Xplorer
- PASPORT pH sensor
- 3 dropper pipets
- labels
- 10-mL graduated cylinder
- test tube rack
- 2 10-mL test tubes
- distilled water
- hydrochloric acid
- sodium hydroxide solution
- 3 stirring rods
- phenolphthalein solution
- 2 25-mL beakers
- large watch glass
- 100-mL beaker
- hot plate

Skills

Observing, Measuring, Analyzing Data

Procedure

Part A: Preparing for the Experiment

1. Plug the USB link into the computer's USB port.
2. Plug the pH sensor into the USB link or Xplorer.

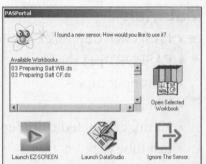

To Computer or
USB Hub ⟶

This will automatically launch the PASPortal window if you are connected to a computer.

3. Choose the appropriate electronic workbook or DataStudio configuration file.

   - If you are using the PASCO electronic workbook specifically designed for this activity, then simply click on the workbook entitled

   ### 03 Preparing Salt WB.ds

   Click on Open Selected Workbook in the PASPortal window and go!

   - If you are not using an electronic workbook, then click on the file entitled

   ### 03 Preparing Salt CF.ds

   Click on Open Selected Workbook in the PASPortal window and proceed with the following instructions.

4. Place about 10 mL of distilled water in a 25-mL beaker. Set the graduated cylinder on the table and add distilled water to the 5-mL mark. Be sure that the *bottom* of the menicus is on the 5 mL line.

5. To determine the number of drops in 1 mL, use a clean dropper pipet to add 1 mL of water to the graduated cylinder. Hold the dropper pipet straight up and down with the tip of the dropper pipet just inside the mouth of the cylinder. As your partner watches the liquid level in the cylinder, add drops of water one at a time while counting the drops. Continue adding drops until the liquid level reaches 6 mL. Record the number of drops in 1 mL in the data table at the end of the lab.

6. Label one clean dropper pipet *Hydrochloric acid (HCl)* and the other *Sodium hydroxide (NaOH)*.

7. Using the HCl dropper pipet, add 3 mL of hydrochloric acid to a clean test tube. **CAUTION** *Hydrochloric acid is corrosive. In case of spills, wash thoroughly with water.* Add 2 to 3 drops of phenolphthalein to the test tube. Use a clean stirring rod to mix the hydrochloric acid and indicator. Record your observations.

8. Using the dropper pipet labeled NaOH, add 3 mL of sodium hydroxide solution to a clean test tube. **CAUTION** *Sodium hydroxide is corrosive. In case of spills, wash thoroughly with water.* Add 2 to 3 drops of phenolphthalein to the test tube. Use a clean stirring rod to mix the sodium hydroxide solution and indicator. Record your observations.

Part B: Making the Salt

9. Using the HCl dropper pipet, add 4 mL of hydrochloric acid to a clean 25-mL beaker. Record the number of drops you used. Add 2 to 4 drops of phenolphthalein to the beaker.

10. Use the NaOH dropper pipet to add sodium hydroxide drop by drop to the beaker of hydrochloric acid and phenolphthalein, stirring constantly. Count the drops as you add them. As a pink color remains longer, add the drops more slowly.

11. Continue to add and count the drops of sodium hydroxide until a light pink color remains for at least 30 seconds. (*Note:* If you add too much sodium hydroxide, add a few more drops of hydrochloric acid until the color disappears. Record any additional drops of hydrochloric acid that you added.) Then, carefully add sodium hydroxide until one drop produces a lasting pink color. Record the total number of drops of sodium hydroxide used.

12. Click on ▶ Start in the DataStudio tool bar if you are connected to a computer.

13. Use the pH probe to determine the pH of the final solution. Record the pH. If the pH is higher than 7.0, add hydrochloric acid solution drop by drop, gently stirring the solution with the pH probe after each drop, until the pH is equal to 7.0. Record the pH and the total number of drops of HCl you added.

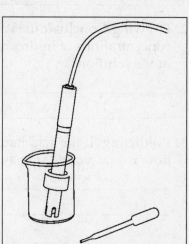

14. Click on ■ Stop in the DataStudio toolbar to end data collection.

15. Pour the solution from the beaker into the watch glass.

16. Fill the 100-mL beaker about half full of water. Place the beaker on top of the hot plate.

17. Set the watch glass on top of the beaker.

18. Turn on the hot plate to a low setting. Adjust the heat as the water in the beaker warms. The water should simmer, but not boil. **CAUTION** *Do not touch the hot plate or the beaker.* Heat until a solid is visible at the edges of the water in the watch glass and the water is nearly evaporated. Turn off the heat.

19. Allow the remaining water to evaporate. Observe the contents of the watch glass. Record your observations.

20. When the watch glass has cooled, dispose of the contents as directed by your teacher. Clean up your equipment. Wash your hands with soap and water.

Data Table

Material(s)	Observation
1 ml	_____ drops
HCl + phenolphthalein	_____ (color)
NaOH + phenolphthalein	_____ (color)
Drops of HCl used	_____ drops
mL of HCl used	_____ mL
Drops of NaOH used	_____ drops
mL of NaOH used	_____ mL
pH of final solution	

Analyze and Conclude

1. **Comparing and Contrasting** What was the total amount (mL) of hydrochloric acid used to make the neutral solution? What was the total amount (mL) of sodium hydroxide? How do the amounts compare?

   _____

   _____

   _____

2. **Drawing Conclusions** What do you conclude about the concentrations of hydrochloric acid and sodium hydroxide in the solutions?

   _____

   _____

3. **Predicting** If the acid had been twice as concentrated as the base, how would your data have changed?

   _____

   _____

Exploration Lab

Investigating a Balloon Jet

In this lab, you will examine the relationships among force, mass, and motion.

Problem

How does a jet-powered device move?

Materials

- PASPORT motion sensor
- PASPORT USB link or Xplorer
- 2 fishing lines, 3 m in length
- 2 drinking straws
- 4 balloons
- masking tape
- meter stick
- 2 threaded nuts
- 2 chairs
- cardboard rectangle (about 6 cm × 20 cm)
- support stand
- disposable pipet

Skills

Applying Concepts

Procedure 🗐

1. Plug the USB link into the computer's USB port or use the Xplorer.
2. Plug the motion sensor into the USB link or the Xplorer.

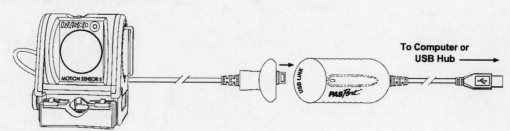

This will automatically launch the PASPortal window.

3. Choose the appropriate electronic workbook or DataStudio configuration file.

   ■ If you are using the PASCO electronic workbook specifically designed for this activity, then simply click on the workbook entitled

   ### 04 Balloon Jet WB.ds

   Click on the Open Selected Workbook icon in the PASPortal window and go!

   ■ If you are not using an electronic workbook, then click on the file entitled

   ### 04 Balloon Jet CF.ds

   Click on the Open Selected Workbook icon in the PASPortal window and proceed with the following instructions.

4. Record your trial results in the data table.

5. Insert the fishing lines through the straws and tie one end of a fishing line to a point on the back of a chair at least 15 cm above the floor. Tie one end of the second fishing line to a point 5 cm from the first line. Tie the other ends of the fishing lines to the other chair in the same way. Pull the chairs apart until the fishing lines are tight and horizontal.

6. Fold the cardboard rectangle in the middle to form a right angle. Tape the cardboard to the straws as shown. The cardboard will act as a target for the motion sensor.

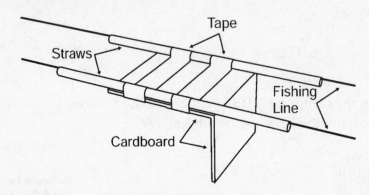

7. Set the switch on top of the motion sensor to the Short Range (cart) setting.

8. Attach the motion sensor to the support stand. Place the support stand on the floor near one end of the fishing line, with the gold disk of the motion sensor aimed at the cardboard rectangle.

9. Slide the balloon sled to the opposite end of the string from the motion sensor.

10. Cut the top and part of the stem off of a disposable pipet as shown.

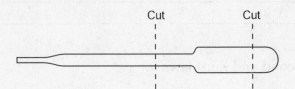

The middle part will be used as a nozzle for the balloon jet. Stretch the opening of the balloon over the nozzle as shown.

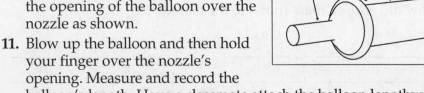

11. Blow up the balloon and then hold your finger over the nozzle's opening. Measure and record the balloon's length. Have a classmate attach the balloon lengthwise to the top of the cardboard using tape.

12. Continue to hold your finger over the nozzle's opening. If you are collecting Data using the DataStudio window, click on ► Start on the toolbar and release the balloon. When the balloon has stopped, click on ■ Stop to end data collection. This is run #1. The average (mean) velocity of the run will appear in the legend of the graph. Record the average velocity in the data table.

13. Repeat Steps 9 through 12 with a new balloon. Make sure to inflate the balloon to the same size as in Step 11. This is run #2. Record the average (mean) velocity in the data table.

14. Repeat Steps 9 through 12 twice more using new balloons. For these runs, tape two nuts to the cardboard before releasing it. The average (mean) velocity of each run will appear in the legend of the graph. Record each average velocity in the data table.

Data Table

Number of Nuts Used	Trial Number	Average Velocity (cm/s)
0	1	
0	2	
2	1	
2	2	
Length of Inflated Balloon (cm)		

Analyze and Conclude

1. **Applying Concepts** Use Newton's second and third laws to explain the motion of the balloon jet.

   _____

   _____

2. **Analyzing Data** How did adding mass (nuts) to the balloon jet affect its motion?

   _____

   _____

Exploration Lab

Determining Buoyant Force

In this lab, you will analyze recorded data to determine the buoyant forces acting on objects.

Problem

How does the buoyant force determine whether an object sinks?

Materials

- PASPORT USB link or Xplorer
- PASPORT force sensor
- string
- rock
- can
- plastic tub
- sponge
- paper towels
- 100-g standard mass
- wooden block tied to a fishing weight
- 250-mL graduated cylinder

Skills

Measuring, Calculating

Procedure

1. Plug the USB link into the computer's USB port or use the Xplorer.
2. Plug the force sensor into the USB link or Xplorer.

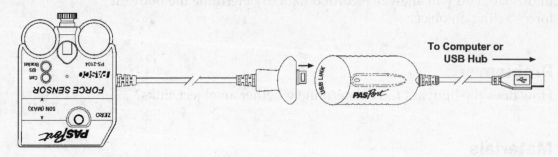

This will automatically launch the PASPortal window if you are
connected to a computer.

3. Choose the appropriate electronic workbook or
   DataStudio configuration file.

   - If you are using the PASCO electronic workbook
     specifically designed for this activity, then simply
     click on the workbook entitled

     05 Buoyant Force WB.ds

     Click on the Open Selected Workbook icon in the
     PASPortal window and go!

   - If you are not using an electronic workbook,
     then click on the file entitled

     05 Buoyant Force CF.ds

     Click on the Open Selected Workbook icon in the PASPortal
     window and proceed with the following instructions.

4. Record your data in the table provided in the lab.

5. Be sure the hook attachment is installed on the force sensor. See the
   Quick Start Card supplied with the sensor for details.

6. Hold the force sensor in a vertical position
   with the hook facing down. With nothing
   hanging from the force sensor, press the
   Zero button on the sensor as shown.

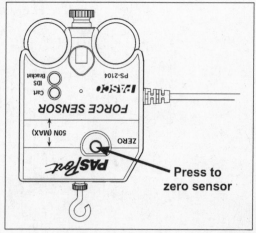

7. Place the can in an upright position in the plastic tub. Completely fill the can with water. Wipe up any water that has spilled into the tub. **CAUTION** *Wipe up any water that spills on the floor to avoid slips and falls.*

8. Tie one end of the string around the rock. Tie the other end to the hook on the force sensor. If you are collecting data using the DataStudio window, click on ► Start on the toolbar. Suspend the rock from the force sensor. The weight of the rock will appear in the digits display in the DataStudio window. Record the rock's weight in air in your data table.

9. Lower the rock into the water in the can until it is completely submerged. Some water may spill from the can into the tub. In your data table, record the apparent weight in water of the submerged rock. Remove the rock from the can.

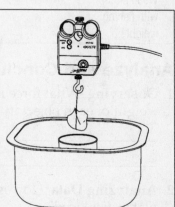

10. If you are using the DataStudio window, click on ■ Stop on the DataStudio toolbar to end data collection.

11. Without spilling any water, carefully remove the can from the tub. Pour the water from the tub into the graduated cylinder. Record the volume of displaced water in your data table.

12. Empty the water from the graduated cylinder.

13. Repeat Steps 8 through 12, first with the 100-g standard mass and then with the wooden block that is tied to a fishing weight.

14. To determine the buoyant force on each object, subtract its apparent weight in water from its weight in air. Record these values.

15. Calculate the weight of the water each object displaces. (*Hint:* 1.0 mL of water has a weight of 0.0098 N.) Record these weights.

Data Table

Object	Weight in Air (N)	Apparent Weight in Water (N)	Buoyant Force (weight in air – apparent weight in water, N)	Volume of Displaced Water (mL)	Weight of Displaced Water (N)
Rock					
100-g standard mass					
Wood block with fishing weight					

Analyze and Conclude

1. Observing What force is responsible for the difference between the weight of each object in the air and its apparent weight in water?

_____

_____

2. Analyzing Data How is the buoyant force related to the weight of water displaced?

_____

_____

3. Forming Operational Definitions Define buoyant force and describe two ways you can measure it or calculate it.

_____

_____

_____

4. Drawing Conclusions Explain what causes an object to sink or to float, using the terms *buoyancy, weight, force, density,* and *gravity.*

_____

_____

_____

Application Lab

Investigating a Spring Clip

There are many ways to use potential energy. A spring clip is a device used to hold weights on a barbell. The spring clip stores energy when you compress it. In this lab, you will determine how the distance you compress a spring clip is related to the force you apply and to the spring's potential energy.

Problem

How does the force you apply to a spring clip affect its elastic potential energy?

Materials

- PASPORT USB link
- PASPORT force sensor
- clamp
- spring clip
- heavy twine
- metric ruler
- graph paper

Skills

Measuring, Using Tables and Graphs

Procedure 🖉 🖾

1. Plug the USB link into the computer's USB port.
2. Plug the force sensor into the USB link or Xplorer.

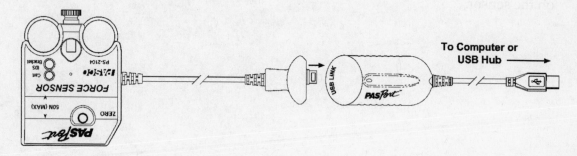

This will automatically launch the PASPortal window.

3. Choose the appropriate electronic workbook or
   DataStudio configuration file.

   ▪ If you are using the PASCO electronic workbook
     specifically designed for this activity, then simply
     click on the workbook entitled

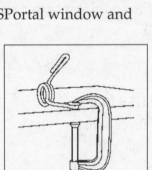

06 Spring Clip WB.ds

   Click on Open Selected Workbook in the
   PASPortal window and go!

   ▪ If you are not using an electronic workbook,
     then click on the file entitled

06 Spring Clip CF.ds

   Click on Open Selected Workbook in the PASPortal window and
   proceed with the following instructions

4. Using the clamp, firmly attach one handle of
   the spring clip to a tabletop, with the other
   handle facing up and away from the table as
   shown. **CAUTION** *Be careful not to pinch
   your fingers with the clamp or spring clip.*

5. Tie a piece of strong twine to the upper
   handle of the spring clip and tie the other
   end of the twine to the hook on the
   force sensor.

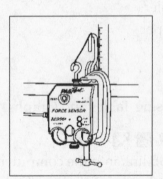

6. Have a classmate hold a metric ruler next to
   the spring clip as shown. Have your teacher
   check your setup for safety before you
   proceed any further. Read the height of the
   upper handle of the spring clip. Record the
   measurement in the data table at the end of
   the lab.

7. Before taking a force measurement, hold
   the sensor in the position it will be in when
   you take the measurement, but without
   pulling on the twine. Press the Zero button
   on the sensor.

8. Click on ► Start on the DataStudio toolbar to begin data collection if you are connected to a computer.

9. Slowly pull the force sensor down at a right angle to the upper handle until the handle moves about 0.1 cm. Record in your data table the force indicated on the digits display on the DataStudio screen and the height of the upper handle. Slowly release the sensor.

10. Repeat Step 9, this time pulling the handle 0.2 cm from the starting position.

11. Continue to repeat step 9, pulling the handle 0.1 cm farther each time. Continue to pull on the handle until the force sensor reaches its maximum force (50 N) or you cannot squeeze the spring clip any farther. You may need to add more rows to the end of your data table for recording handle position and force.

12. Click on ■ Stop to end data collection.

13. Graph your data. Place the distance the handle moved on the horizontal axis and the force applied on the vertical axis.

Analyze and Conclude

1. **Using Graphs** What is the approximate relationship between the total distance you compressed the spring clip and the force you applied to it?

_____

_____

_____

2. **Classifying** What type of energy transfer did you use to compress the spring clip? What type of energy did the spring clip gain when it was compressed?

_____

_____

_____

3. **Drawing Conclusions** What relationship exists between the distance the spring clip was compressed and its potential energy? (*Hint:* The elastic potential energy of the spring equals the work done on it.)

_____

_____

Data Table

Total Distance Moved (cm)	Position of Handle (cm)	Force (N)
0.0 cm		
0.1 cm		
0.2 cm		
0.3 cm		
0.4 cm		
0.5 cm		
0.6 cm		
0.7 cm		
0.8 cm		
0.9 cm		
1.0 cm		
1.1 cm		
1.2 cm		
1.3 cm		
1.4 cm		
1.5 cm		
1.6 cm		
1.7 cm		
1.8 cm		
1.9 cm		
2.0 cm		
2.1 cm		
2.2 cm		
2.3 cm		
2.4 cm		
2.5 cm		

Design Your Own Lab

Using Specific Heat to Analyze Metals

In this lab, you will determine the specific heat of steel and of aluminum. Then you will use specific heat to analyze the composition of a metal can.

Problem

How can you use specific heat to determine the composition of a metal can?

Materials

- PASPORT USB link or Xplorer
- PASPORT temperature sensor
- 10 steel bolts
- balance
- 50-cm length of string
- clamp
- ring stand
- boiling water bath
- 500-mL graduated cylinder
- ice water
- foam cup with lid
- aluminum nails
- crushed can

Skills

Calculating, Designing Experiments

Procedure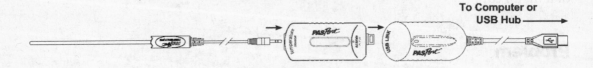

Part A: Determining Specific Heat

1. Plug the USB link into the computer's USB port or use an Xplorer.
2. Plug the temperature sensor into the USB link or the Xplorer.

To Computer or USB Hub →

This will automatically launch the PASPortal window if you are connected to the computer.

3. Choose the appropriate electronic workbook or DataStudio configuration file.

   - If you are using the PASCO electronic workbook specifically designed for this activity, then simply click on the workbook entitled

     07 Specific Heat-Metals WB.ds

     Click on the Open Selected Workbook icon in the PASPortal window and go!

   - If you are not using an electronic workbook, then click on the file entitled

     07 Specific Heat-Metals CF.ds

     Click on the Open Selected Workbook icon in the PASPortal window and proceed with the following instructions.

4. Use the data table at the end of the lab to record your data.
5. Measure the mass of 10 steel bolts and record it in your data table.
6. Tie one end of the string to all 10 bolts. Use a clamp and ring stand to suspend the bolts in the boiling water bath. **CAUTION** *Be careful not to splash boiling water.* Make sure the temperature sensor is in the boiling water bath but not touching the bottom of the beaker. After a few minutes, select Monitor Data from the Experiment menu on the DataStudio menu bar. The temperature of the water will appear in the digits display on the computer screen. Record the water temperature as the initial temperature of the bolts.

Select Monitor Data from the Experiment Menu

7. Click on ■ Stop to end the data monitoring in the DataStudio window.

8. Use a graduated cylinder to pour 200 mL of ice water (without ice) into the foam cup. Using the temperature sensor, measure and record the temperature of the ice water. Record the mass of the ice water. (*Hint:* The density of water is 1 g/mL.)

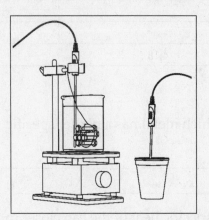

9. Use the clamp to move the bolts into the cup of ice water. Cover the cup and insert your temperature sensor through the hole in the cover. Select Monitor Data from the Experiment menu on the DataStudio menu bar. The temperature of the water will appear in the digits display on the computer screen.

Select Monitor Data from the Experiment Menu

10. Gently swirl the water in the cup. Observe the temperature until it stops rising.

11. Click on ■ Stop to end data monitoring in the DataStudio window. Record the highest temperature as the final temperature for both the water and the steel bolts.

12. Calculate and record the specific heat of steel. (*Hint:* Use the equation $Q = m \times c \times \Delta T$ to calculate the energy the water absorbs.)

13. Repeat Steps 5 through 12 with aluminum nails to determine the specific heat of aluminum. Start by making a new data table. Use a mass of aluminum that is close to the mass you used for the steel bolts.

Part B: Design Your Own Experiment

14. **Designing Experiments** Design an experiment that uses specific heat to identify the metals a can might be made of.

15. After your teacher approves your plan, perform your experiment.

Data Table

Measurement	Water	Steel Bolt
Mass (g)		
Initial temperature (°C)		
Final temperature (°C)		
Specific heat (J/g·°C)	4.18	

Analyze and Conclude

1. **Comparing and Contrasting** Which metal has a higher specific heat, aluminum or steel?

   _____

   _____

2. **Drawing Conclusions** Was the specific heat of the can closer to the specific heat of steel or of aluminum? What can you conclude about the material in the can?

   _____

   _____

3. **Evaluating** Did your observations prove what the can was made of? If not, what other information would you need to be sure?

   _____

   _____

   _____

4. **Inferring** The can you used is often called a tin can. The specific heat of tin is 0.23 J/g·°C. Did your data support the idea that the can was made mostly of tin? Explain your answer.

   _____

   _____

   _____

Forensics Lab

Evaluating Electrical Safety

Electrical appliances must be safely insulated to protect users from injury. In this lab, you will play the role of a safety engineer determining whether an electric power supply is safely insulated.

Problem

How much resistance is needed in series with a known resistance to reduce the voltage by 99 percent?

Materials

- PASPORT voltage and current sensor
- PASPORT USB link or Xplorer
- 9-volt battery
- battery clip
- 3 alligator clips
- 4 resistors: 1 ohm, 10 ohms, 100 ohms, 1000 ohms

Skills

Calculating, Using Tables

Procedure 🐾 🎬 📋 ✂️

1. Plug the USB link into the computer's USB port or use the Xplorer.
2. Plug the voltage and current sensor into the USB link or the Xplorer.

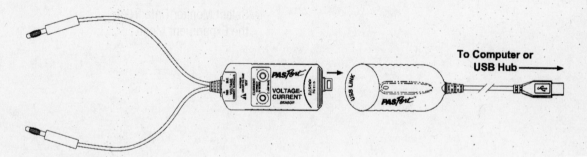

To Computer or
USB Hub →

This will automatically launch the PASPortal window if you are connected to a computer.

3. Choose the appropriate electronic workbook or DataStudio configuration file.

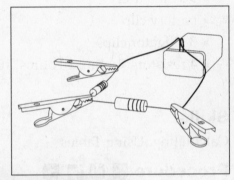

- If you are using the PASCO electronic workbook specifically designed for this activity, then simply click on the workbook entitled

  08 Electrical Safety WB.ds

  Click on the Open Selected Workbook icon in the PASPortal window and go!

- If you are not using an electronic workbook, then click on the file entitled

  08 Electrical Safety CF.ds

  Click on the Open Selected Workbook icon in the PASPortal window and proceed with the following instructions.

4. Use the data table at the end of the lab to record your voltage readings.

5. Attach the battery clip to the battery. **CAUTION** *The circuit may become hot.*

6. Use an alligator clip to attach one wire of the 1-ohm resistor to one of the battery clip's wires as shown.

7. Clip one wire of the 1000-ohm resistor to the free end of the 1-ohm resistor. Clip the other wire of the 1000-ohm resistor to the free wire of the battery clip. The 1-ohm resistor represents the current-carrying part of the appliance. The 1000-ohm resistor represents the insulation for the current-carrying part.

8. Select Monitor Data from the Experiment menu on the DataStudio menu bar.

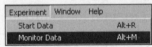

Select Monitor Data from the Experiment Menu

9. Place one of the voltage and current sensor's voltage electrodes on each wire of the 1-ohm resistor. Record the voltage difference.

10. Place the voltage and current sensor's voltage electrodes on the wires of the 1000-ohm resistor. Record the voltage difference.

11. To model a reduction in the resistance of the insulation, repeat Steps 7 through 10, replacing the 1000-ohm resistor with the 100-ohm resistor. Disconnect the resistors from the battery clip.

12. **Predicting** Record your prediction of how increasing the resistance of the current-carrying part of an appliance will affect the voltage difference across the insulating part.

13. To test your prediction, repeat Steps 6 through 11, using the 10-ohm resistor to represent the current-carrying part of the appliance.

14. Click on ■ Stop on the toolbar to end data monitoring in the DataStudio window.

Data Table

Current-Carrying Resistance (ohms)	Insulating Resistance (ohms)	Current-Carrying Voltage Difference (volts)	Insulating Voltage Difference (volts)
1	1000		
1	100		
10	1000		
10	100		

Analyze and Conclude

1. **Calculating** When the resistance of the current-carrying part was 1 ohm and the resistance of the insulating part was 100 ohms, what was the ratio of the voltage differences across the current-carrying part and the insulating part?

   _____

   _____

2. **Drawing Conclusions** In the circuit you built, what is the voltage difference across each resistor proportional to?

   _____

   _____

3. **Applying Concepts** If you know the resistance of the current-carrying part of an appliance, what should the resistance of the insulation be to reduce the voltage by 99 percent?

   _____

   _____

Application Lab

Investigating an Electric Generator

All generators have two main parts—a magnet and a wire that is wrapped into many coils. Usually, one of these parts remains in place as the other moves. The arrangement of these parts varies, depending on the size and power of the generator and whether it produces direct or alternating current. In this lab, you will determine how several variables affect the current produced by a simple generator.

Problem

How do the direction in which the magnet moves and the number and direction of the wire coil windings affect the current that a generator produces?

Materials

- PASPORT USB link or Xplorer
- PASPORT voltage and current sensor
- patch cords and alligator clips (supplied with voltage and current sensor)
- 5-m length of insulated wire
- cardboard tube
- notepad or soft-cover book
- bar magnet
- metric ruler
- tape
- graph paper

Skills

Observing, Using Graphs

Procedure 🔬 🧪

Part A: Changing the Number of Coils

1. Plug the USB link into the computer's USB port or use the Xplorer.
2. Plug the red patch cord into the positive (+) socket on the voltage and current sensor.
3. Plug the black patch cord into the negative (−) socket on the voltage and current sensor.

4. Put the alligator clips on the free ends of the patch cords.

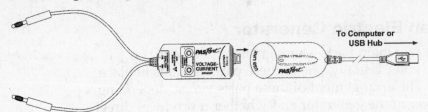

5. Plug the voltage and current sensor into the USB link or the Xplorer. This will automatically launch the PASPortal window if you are connected to a computer.

6. Choose the appropriate electronic workbook or DataStudio configuration file.

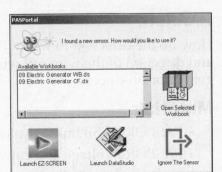

- If you are using the PASCO electronic workbook specifically designed for this activity, then simply click on the workbook entitled

09 Electric Generator WB.ds

  Click on the Open Selected Workbook icon in the PASPortal window and go!

- If you are not using an electronic workbook, then click on the file entitled

09 Electric Generator CF.ds

  Click on the Open Selected Workbook icon in the PASPortal window and proceed with the following instructions.

7. Slip the insulated wire between your hand and the cardboard tube so that 15 cm of wire extends from the tube. Use a piece of tape to hold the wire in place on the tube. Use your other hand to wrap the long end of the wire around the tube 10 times in a clockwise direction, as shown. Make sure that all of the coils are within 10 cm of the end of the tube. **CAUTION** *Be careful not to cut yourself on the*

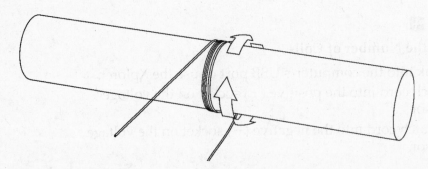

sharp ends of the wire.

8. Connect the free end of the red patch cord to the end of the wire that is closer to the coils. Connect the free end of the black patch cord to the end of the wire that is farther from the coils.

9. Hold the cardboard tube vertically over a notepad or soft-cover book with the red patch cord at the bottom of the coil. The pad will act as a landing pad for the magnet.

Chapter 21   **Lab 9**

10. Hold the bar magnet by its south pole. Position the magnet so that the end closest to the tube is even with the top of the tube.

11. If you are collecting data using the DataStudio window, click on ▶ Start on the toolbar.

12. Observe the current display on the screen as you drop the bar magnet into the open end of the cardboard.

13. Click on ■ Stop on the DataStudio toolbar to end data collection in the DataStudio window.

14. In DataStudio, the data will be displayed in a graph. Use the mouse cursor to draw a box around the portion of the graph that shows the greatest change in current. Click on the Scale to Fit button on the graph toolbar.

Scale to Fit

Smart Tool

15. Use the Smart Tool on the Graph toolbar in DataStudio to find the first (left) part of the graph that shows the greatest change in current.

16. Record the maximum current in the data table at the end of the lab.

17. Disconnect the black patch cord from the end of the wire that is farther from the coils.

18. **Predicting** Record your prediction of how increasing the number of wire coils will affect the current.

19. To test your prediction, wrap the wire around the tube 10 more times in the same direction that you wound it previously— clockwise. You should now have a total of 20 coils. Reconnect the black patch cord to the wire.

20. Repeat Steps 10–16.

21. Again, disconnect the black patch cord from the same end of the wire. Wrap the wire clockwise around the tube 10 more times for a total of 30 coils. Reconnect the patch cord to the wire.

22. Repeat Steps 10–16.

Part B: Changing Other Properties of the Generator

23. **Predicting** Record you prediction of how reversing the direction of the magnet will affect the current.

24. To test your prediction, repeat Steps 10–16, but this time, hold the magnet by its north pole.

25. **Predicting** Record your prediction of how reversing the direction of the wire coils will affect the current if you hold the magnet by its south pole.

26. To test your prediction, disconnect the voltage and current sensor from the wire. Unwind the wire coils. Rewind the wire around the tube 30 times holding the tube and the wire as you did in step 7, but winding the insulated wire in the opposite direction— counterclockwise. Reconnect the red patch cord to the insulated wire extending from the bottom of the coils. Reconnect the black patch cord to the wire extending from the top of the coils.

27. Repeat Steps 10–16.

28. Construct a graph using the data from the first three rows in your
    data table. Plot the number of coils on the horizontal axis and the
    current on the vertical axis.

Data Tables

Number of Coils	Direction of Coils	Pole Inserted	Current (A)
10	Clockwise	North	
20	Clockwise	North	
30	Clockwise	North	
30	Clockwise	South	
30	Counterclockwise	North	

Prediction 1	
Prediction 2	
Prediction 3	

Analyze and Conclude

1. **Inferring** What caused the current to flow in the wire?

   _____

   _____

2. **Using Graphs** Based on your graph, what is the relationship
   between the number of coils and the amount of current?

   _____

   _____

3. **Analyzing Data** Explain the effect that reversing the direction of
   the magnet or the coils had on the direction of the current.

   _____

   _____

4. **Predicting** Explain whether a generator could be built with a
   stationary magnet and wire coils that moved.

   _____

   _____

   _____

5. **Evaluating and Revising** Did your observations support your
   predictions? If not, evaluate any flaws in the reasoning you used to
   make the predictions.

   _____

   _____

Exploration Lab

Determining Relative Humidity

To measure relative humidity, you can use two temperature sensors. An absorbent wick keeps the bulb of one temperature sensor wet. When air flows over the wet bulb, the rate of evaporation increases. In this lab, you will discover how two temperature sensors measure the relative humidity of the surrounding air.

Problem

How can you measure the relative humidity of the air?

Materials

- 2 PASPORT USB links
- 2 PASPORT temperature sensors
- PASPORT humidity sensor (optional)
- cardboard rectangle
- absorbent wick (gauze or flat shoe lace)

Skills

Using Tables, Formulating Hypotheses

Procedure 🖳 🗄 🔧 🌾 🖐

1. Plug the USB links into the computer's USB ports or a USB hub.
2. Plug one of the temperature sensors into a USB link or Xplorer. This will be sensor #1.

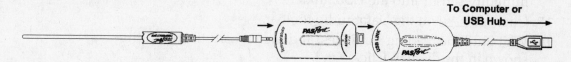

To Computer or USB Hub →

   This will automatically launch the PASPortal window.

3. Choose the appropriate electronic workbook or DataStudio configuration file.
   - If you are going to use the PASCO electronic workbook specifically designed for this activity, then simply click on the workbook entitled

10 Relative Humidity WB.ds

   Click on Open Selected Workbook in the PASPortal window and go!

   - If you are not using an electronic workbook, then click on the file entitled

10 Relative Humidity CF.ds

   Click on Open Selected Workbook in the PASPortal window and proceed with the following instructions.

4. Plug the other temperature sensor into the other USB link. This will be sensor #2.

5. Put the absorbent wick on the end of temperature sensor #2.

6. Moisten the absorbent wick on sensor #2 with room-temperature water.

7. Place the two temperature sensors next to each other at the edge of a table with the ends extending over the edge.

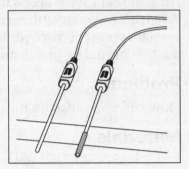

8. Click on ▶ Start on the DataStudio toolbar if you are connected to the computer.

9. Observe the temperature readings as you use the cardboard rectangle to vigorously fan the ends of the temperature probes.

10. Continue to fan until the temperature of the wet-bulb temperature sensor remains constant. Then, record the temperatures of both temperature sensors in the data table at the end of the lab.

11. Click on ■ Stop to end data collection.

12. Calculate the difference between your dry-bulb and wet-bulb temperatures.

13. In the relative humidity chart at the end of the lab, find the row that lists the dry-bulb temperature that you recorded. Then find the column that lists the difference in temperature that you calculated. The number located where this row and column meet is the relative humidity of the classroom. Record the relative humidity in your data table.

14. Unplug one of the temperature sensors and plug the PASPORT humidity sensor into the USB link.

15. Click on ▶ Start on the DataStudio toolbar.

16. Wait until the reading stabilizes, and then record the humidity shown in the display. Click ■ Stop.

17. With your teacher's approval, use the humidity sensor to measure the relative humidity at a different location.

Relative Humidity Chart

To find the relative humidity, measure the wet-bulb and dry-bulb temperatures with a sling psychrometer. Find the dry-bulb reading in the left column and the difference between readings at the top of the table. The number where these readings intersect is the relative humidity in percent.

Relative Humidity (percent)														
Dry-Bulb Reading (°C)	Difference Between Wet-Bulb and Dry-Bulb Readings (°C)													
	1	2	3	4	5	6	7	8	9	10	11	12	13	14
5	86	72	58	45	33	20	7							
6	86	73	60	48	35	24	11							
7	87	74	62	50	38	26	15							
8	87	75	63	51	40	29	19	8						
9	88	76	64	53	42	32	22	12						
10	88	77	66	55	44	34	24	15	6					
11	89	78	67	56	46	36	27	18	9					
12	89	78	68	58	48	39	29	21	12					
13	89	79	69	59	50	41	32	23	15	7				
14	90	79	70	60	51	42	34	26	18	10				
15	90	80	71	61	53	44	36	27	20	13	6			
16	90	81	71	63	54	46	38	30	23	15	8			
17	90	81	72	64	55	47	40	32	25	18	11			
18	91	82	73	65	57	49	41	34	27	20	14	7		
19	91	82	74	65	58	50	43	36	29	22	16	10		
20	91	83	74	66	59	51	44	37	31	24	18	12	6	
21	91	83	75	67	60	53	46	39	32	26	20	14	9	
22	92	83	76	68	61	54	47	40	34	28	22	17	11	6
23	92	84	76	69	62	55	48	42	36	30	24	19	13	8
24	92	84	77	69	62	56	49	43	37	31	26	20	15	10
25	92	84	77	70	63	57	50	44	39	33	28	22	17	12
26	92	85	78	71	64	58	51	46	40	34	29	24	19	14
27	92	85	78	71	65	58	52	47	41	36	31	26	21	16
28	93	85	78	72	65	59	53	48	42	37	32	27	22	18
29	93	86	79	72	66	60	54	49	43	38	33	28	24	19
30	93	86	79	73	67	61	55	50	44	39	35	30	25	21

Data Table

Location	Dry-Bulb Temp. (°C)	Wet-Bulb Temp. (°C)	Relative Humidity From Chart (%)	Relative Humidity From Sensor (%)
Classroom				

Analyze and Conclude

1. **Analyzing Data** Why did the two temperature sensors have different temperatures?

_____

_____

_____

_____

2. **Formulating Hypotheses** Explain how the relative humidity of the air affected the difference between the temperatures of the two temperature sensors.

_____

_____

_____

3. **Drawing Conclusions** What do you think caused the difference in relative humidity between the two locations?

_____

_____

4. **Predicting** How would the relative humidity change if you cooled the air in the classroom?

_____

_____

_____

5. **Evaluating** Is there a difference in the relative humidity measured by the sensor and the relative humidity you found with the temperature sensors and the chart? If so, explain what may have caused the difference.

_____

_____

Go Further

Measure and record the temperature and relative humidity outside your school or at home at various times of the day for several days. Graph these data and explain any patterns that you observe.

Contents

Vernier Lab

Textbook Correlation

1. Investigating Changes in Temperature During Heating of Solids — Exploration Lab, p. 92 — 44
2. Predicting the Density of an Element — Exploration Lab, p. 150 — 47
3. Preparing a Salt by Neutralization — Exploration Lab, p. 254 — 51
4. Investigating a Balloon Jet — Exploration Lab, p. 383 — 55
5. Determining Buoyant Force — Exploration Lab, p. 405 — 58
6. Investigating a Spring Clip — Application Lab, p. 467 — 61
7. Using Specific Heat to Analyze Metals — Design Your Own Lab, p. 493 — 64
8. Evaluating Electrical Safety — Forensics Lab, p. 623 — 67
9. Investigating an Electric Generator — Application Lab, p. 648 — 70
10. Determining Relative Humidity — Exploration Lab, p. 783 — 74

Teacher Notes and Answers

Vernier Labs — 123

Exploration Lab

Investigating Changes in Temperature During Heating of Solids

Lauric acid is a solid that is found in coconuts and processed foods that are made with coconut oil. Lauric acid is also used to make some soaps and cosmetics. In this lab, you will measure the temperature of ice and of lauric acid as these solids are heated and melt. You will graph the data you collect and compare the heating curves for ice and for lauric acid.

Problem

What happens to the temperature of a substance during a phase change?

Materials

- LabPro interface
- Logger *Pro* software
- Vernier stainless steel temperature probe
- 500-mL beaker
- crushed ice
- hot plate
- clock with second hand
- test tube of lauric acid with a stainless steel temperature probe
- glass stirring rod
- graph paper

Skills

Measuring, Using Graphs

Procedure 🖾 🖾 🖾 🖾 🖾

Part A: Heating Ice

1. Use the data table found at the end of the lab to record your data. You may need to add more rows to the end of your data table if the solids do not melt within 20 minutes.
2. Connect the stainless steel temperature probe into Channel 1 of the LabPro.
3. Launch Logger *Pro* and open the Temperature Changes.xmbl file.
4. Logger *Pro* will display the temperature measurement in a meter on the computer screen. If the probe is in air, verify that it reads the correct room temperature.
5. Fill a 500-mL beaker halfway with crushed ice. **CAUTION** *Use care when handling glassware to avoid breakage. Wipe up any spilled ice right away to avoid slips and falls.*

6. Place the beaker on a hot plate. Don't turn the hot plate on yet. Insert the stainless steel temperature probe into the ice. Because it takes several seconds for the probe to adjust to the temperature of its surroundings, wait 20 seconds and then measure the temperature of the ice. Record this temperature next to the 0 minutes entry in your data table.

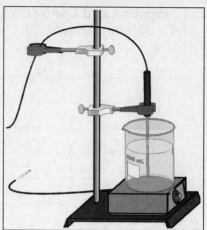

7. Turn the hot plate to a low setting. **CAUTION** *Be careful not to touch the hot plate because it could burn you.*

8. Observe and record the temperature of the water at one-minute intervals until all the ice has changed to liquid water. Circle the temperature at which you first observe liquid water and the temperature at which all the ice has changed to liquid water.

9. After all the ice has melted, make five more measurements of the temperature at one-minute intervals. Turn off the hot plate.

10. Graph your data with time on the horizontal axis and temperature on the vertical axis.

Part B: Heating Lauric Acid

11. Empty the water from the beaker into the sink. Fill the beaker halfway with cool tap water.

12. Place a test tube containing lauric acid and a stainless steel temperature probe into the beaker. If necessary, add or remove water from the beaker so that the surface of the water is above the surface of the lauric acid but below the opening of the test tube.

13. Place the beaker on the hot plate. After 20 seconds, measure the temperature of the lauric acid. Record this temperature next to the 0 minutes entry in your data table.

14. Repeat Steps 7 through 10 using the lauric acid instead of the ice. To keep the temperature the same throughout the water bath, use the glass stirring rod to stir the water after you take each temperature measurement.

Analyze and Conclude

1. **Using Graphs** Describe the shape of your graph for ice.

_____

_____

2. **Analyzing Data** What happened to the temperature of the ice-water mixture during the phase change?

_____

_____

_____

3. **Comparing and Contrasting** Compare the shapes of the graphs for ice and for lauric acid. Compare the melting points of ice and lauric acid.

_____

_____

_____

_____

_____

_____

Data Table

Time (minutes)	Temperature of Water (°C)	Temperature of Lauric Acid (°C)
0		
1		
2		
3		
4		
5		
6		
7		
8		
9		
10		
11		
12		
13		
14		
15		
16		
17		
18		
19		
20		

Exploration Lab

Predicting the Density of an Element

Density is a useful property for identifying and classifying elements. In this lab, you will determine the densities of three elements in Group 4A—silicon, tin, and lead. Then you will use your data to predict the density of another element in Group 4A—germanium.

Problem

Can the densities of elements within a group be used to help predict the density of another element in the group?

Materials

- LabPro interface
- Logger *Pro* software
- Vernier dual-range force sensor
- unlined white paper
- scissors
- metric ruler
- yogurt cup with string
- silicon
- tin
- lead shot
- 50-mL graduated cylinder
- graph paper
- periodic table

Skills

Measuring, Observing, Using Graphs, Calculating

Procedure 🌀 🏠 🔋 ✋ ✂️

Part A: Measuring Mass

1. Cut out three 10-cm × 10-cm pieces of paper from a sheet of unlined white paper. Label one piece of paper Silicon, the second Tin, and the third Lead.

2. Attach the force sensor to a ring stand so that the metal hook on the sensor is pointing toward the floor. Suspend the yogurt cup from the force sensor using the string attached to the cup.

Vernier
Lab 2

3. Connect the dual-range force sensor into Channel 1 of the LabPro interface. Set the switch on the front of the sensor to the lowest setting (± 10 N).

4. Launch Logger *Pro* and open the Density of an Element.xmbl file. Logger *Pro* will display the force measurement in a meter on the computer screen.

5. With the empty cup suspended from the force sensor, click on ⌊ Zero ⌋ to zero the sensor.

6. Monitoring the measurements displayed on the computer screen, pour enough silicon into the cup to reach a force of approximately 0.2 N. Divide the measurement displayed on the computer screen by 0.0098 to calculate the mass of the silicon in grams. Record the mass in the data table at the end of the lab.

7. Empty the silicon from the cup onto the paper labeled Silicon.

8. Repeat Steps 6 and 7 for both tin and lead. (*Tip:* To prevent the lead shot from rolling off the paper, fold the edges of the paper up to form a shallow box.)

Part B: Measuring Volume

9. Place 25 mL of water in the graduated cylinder. Measure the volume of the water to the nearest 0.1 mL. Record the volume (in cm^3) in the data table at the end of the lab. (*Hint:* 1 mL = 1 cm^3)

10. Tilt the graduated cylinder and carefully pour the silicon from the paper into the graduated cylinder. Make sure that the silicon is completely covered by the water. Measure and record the volume of the water and silicon in your data table. Then, subtract the volume of water from the volume of the water and silicon. Record the result in your data table.

11. Repeat Steps 9 and 10 to find the volumes of tin and lead.

Part C: Calculating Density

12. To calculate the density of silicon, divide its mass by its volume.

$$\text{Density} = \frac{\text{Mass}}{\text{Volume}}$$

Record the density of silicon in your data table.

13. Repeat Step 12 to find the densities of tin and lead.

14. Make a line graph that shows the relationship between the densities of silicon, tin, and lead and the periods in which they are located in the periodic table. Place the number of the period (from 1 to 7) on the horizontal axis and the density (in g/cm^3) on the vertical axis. Draw a straight line that comes as close as possible to all three points.

15. Germanium is in Period 4. To estimate the density of germanium, draw a dotted vertical line from the 4 on the horizontal axis to the solid line. Then, draw a dotted horizontal line from the solid line to the vertical axis. Read and record the density of germanium.

16. Wash your hands with warm water and soap before you leave the laboratory.

Data Table

Element	Mass of Element (g)	Volume of Water (cm³)	Volume of Water and Element (cm³)	Volume of Element (cm³)	Density of Element (g/cm³)
Silicon					
Tin					
Lead					

Analyze and Conclude

1. Classifying List lead, silicon, and tin in order of increasing density.

_____

_____

2. Comparing and Contrasting How does your estimate of the density of germanium compare with the actual density of germanium, which is 5.3 g/cm³?

_____

_____

3. Calculating Use the formula for percent error (PE) to calculate a percent error for your estimate of the density of germanium.

$$PE = \frac{\text{Estimated value} - \text{Accepted value}}{\text{Accepted value}} * 100$$

4. Drawing Conclusions How does the density of the elements change from silicon to lead in Group 4A?

_____

_____

Go Further

Use reference books or sites on the Internet to research properties of Group 4A elements. Construct a graph that shows how another property, such as melting point or boiling point, varies among the Group 4A elements you explored. Determine whether knowing the values for three of the elements would allow you to accurately predict a value for the fourth element.

Exploration Lab

Preparing a Salt by Neutralization

In this lab, you will prepare table salt by reacting hydrochloric acid (HCl) with sodium hydroxide (NaOH). To be sure that all of the acid and base have reacted, you will use phenolphthalein. You will first have to test the colors of this indicator with a known acid and base. After the acid and base have reacted, you will measure the pH of the solution with a pH sensor. Finally, you will evaporate the water and collect the sodium chloride.

Problem

How can you produce a salt by neutralization?

Materials

- LabPro interface
- Logger *Pro* software
- Vernier pH sensor
- 3 dropper pipets
- labels
- 10-mL graduated cylinder
- test tube rack
- 2 10-mL test tubes
- distilled water
- hydrochloric acid solution
- sodium hydroxide solution
- 3 stirring rods
- phenolphthalein solution
- 2 25-mL beakers
- large watch glass
- 100-mL beaker
- hot plate

Skills

Observing, Measuring, Analyzing Data

Procedure 🖉 🖐 🔬 🔖 🖐

Part A: Preparing for the Experiment

1. Connect the pH sensor into Channel 1 of the LabPro.

2. Launch Logger *Pro* and open the Preparing Salt.xmbl file.

3. Logger *Pro* will display the pH measurement in a meter on the computer screen.

4. Place about 10 mL of distilled water in a 25-mL beaker. Set the graduated cylinder on the table and add distilled water to the 5-mL mark. Be sure that the *bottom* of the meniscus is on the 5-mL line.

5. To determine the number of drops in 1 mL, use a clean dropper pipet to add 1 mL of water to the graduated cylinder. Hold the dropper pipet straight up and down with the tip of the dropper pipet just inside the mouth of the cylinder. As your partner watches the liquid level in the cylinder, add drops of water one at a time while counting the drops. Continue adding drops until the liquid level reaches 6 mL. Record the number of drops in 1.0 mL in the data table at the end of the lab.

6. Label one clean dropper pipet *Hydrochloric acid (HCl)* and the other *Sodium hydroxide (NaOH)*.

7. Using the HCl dropper pipet, add 3.0 mL of hydrochloric acid to a clean test tube. **CAUTION** *Hydrochloric acid is corrosive. In case of spills, wash thoroughly with water.* Add 2 to 3 drops of phenolphthalein to the test tube. Use a clean stirring rod to mix the hydrochloric acid and indicator. Record your observations.

8. Using the dropper pipet labeled NaOH, add 3.0 mL of sodium hydroxide solution to a clean test tube. **CAUTION** *Sodium hydroxide is corrosive. In case of spills, wash thoroughly with water.* Add 2 to 3 drops of phenolphthalein to the test tube. Use a clean stirring rod to mix the sodium hydroxide solution and indicator. Record your observations.

Part B: Making the Salt

9. Using the HCl dropper pipet, add 4.0 mL of hydrochloric acid to a clean 25-mL beaker. Record the number of drops you used. Add 2 to 4 drops of phenolphthalein to the beaker.

10. Use the NaOH dropper pipet to add sodium hydroxide drop by drop to the beaker of hydrochloric acid and phenolphthalein, stirring constantly. Count the drops as you add them. As a pink color remains longer, add the drops more slowly.

11. Continue to add and count the drops of sodium hydroxide until a light pink color remains for at least 30 seconds. (*Note:* If you add too much sodium hydroxide, add a few more drops of hydrochloric acid until the color disappears. Record any additional drops of hydrochloric acid that you added.) Then, carefully add sodium hydroxide until one drop produces a lasting pink color. Record the total number of drops of sodium hydroxide used.

12. Use the pH sensor to determine the pH of the final solution (the glass bulb at the tip of the probe must be submerged). Record the pH. If the pH is higher than 7.0, add hydrochloric acid drop by drop until the pH is equal to 7.0. Record the pH and the total number of drops of HCl you added.

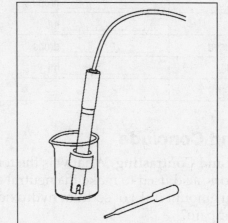

13. Pour the solution from the beaker into the watch glass.

14. Fill the 100-mL beaker about half full of water. Place the beaker on top of the hot plate.

15. Set the watch glass on top of the beaker.

16. Turn on the hot plate to a low setting. Adjust the heat as the water in the beaker warms. The water should simmer, but not boil. **CAUTION** *Do not touch the hot plate or the beaker*. Heat until a solid is visible at the edges of the water in the watch glass and the water is nearly evaporated. Turn off the heat.

17. Allow the remaining water to evaporate. Observe the contents of the watch glass. Record your observations.

18. When the watch glass has cooled, dispose of the contents as directed by your teacher. Clean up your equipment. Wash your hands with soap and water.

Chapter 8   **Lab 3**

Data Table

Material(s)	Observation
1 ml	_____ drops
HCl + phenolphthalein	_____ (color)
NaOH + phenolphthalein	_____ (color)
Drops of HCl used	_____ drops
mL of HCl used	_____ mL
Drops of NaOH used	_____ drops
mL of NaOH used	_____ mL
pH of final solution	

Analyze and Conclude

1. **Comparing and Contrasting** What was the total amount (mL) of hydrochloric acid used to make the neutral solution? What was the total amount (mL) of sodium hydroxide? How do the amounts compare?

_____

_____

_____

2. **Drawing Conclusions** What do you conclude about the concentrations of hydrochloric acid and sodium hydroxide in the solutions?

_____

_____

3. **Predicting** If the acid had been twice as concentrated as the base, how would your data have changed?

_____

_____

Exploration Lab

Investigating a Balloon Jet

In this lab, you will examine the relationships among force, mass, and motion.

Problem

How does a jet-powered device move?

Materials

- LabPro interface
- Logger *Pro* software
- Vernier motion detector
- string, 3 m in length
- drinking straw
- 4 long balloons
- masking tape
- meter stick
- 2 threaded nuts
- 2 chairs

Skills

Applying Concepts

Procedure 🐾

1. Connect the motion detector into the DIG/SONIC 1 port of the LabPro interface.

2. Launch Logger *Pro* and open the Balloon Jet.xmbl file.

3. Logger *Pro* will display the current distance measurement in a meter on the computer screen.

4. Insert the string through the straw and tie each end of the string to the back of a separate chair. Pull the chairs apart until the string is tight and horizontal.

5. Blow up the balloon and then hold the balloon's opening closed. Record the length of the balloon. Have a classmate attach the balloon lengthwise to the straw using tape.

6. While continuing to hold the balloon's opening closed, have your classmate position the balloon jet so that the balloon's opening is 0.5 meters from a chair.

7. Hold up the motion detector next to the chair, aimed at the balloon and in line with the string. When the balloon is released, it should move away from the motion detector.

8. Click on ⟦▶Collect⟧ to begin collecting data, and release the balloon.

9. Click on the Examine button. Move the mouse pointer to the data point that marks the starting movement of the balloon. Note the distance and time values displayed in the examine box. Round to the nearest 0.01 m. Move the mouse pointer to the data point that marks when the balloon stopped moving and note the distance and time.

Examine Button

10. Calculate the total distance traveled by the balloon in the trial by subtracting the starting distance from the final distance. Calculate the total time by subtracting the starting time from the final time. Record your results in the data table for 0 Nuts Used, Trial 1.

11. Repeat Steps 5 through 10 with a new balloon. Make sure to inflate the balloon to the same size as in Step 6. Record your results in the data table for 0 Nuts Used, Trial 2.

12. Repeat Steps 5 through 10 twice more with a new balloons. This time, tape two nuts to each balloon before releasing it. Record your results in the data table for 2 Nuts Used, Trials 1 and 2.

13. Calculate and record the average velocity for each trial. The average velocity is equal to the distance divided by the time.

Data Table

Number of Nuts Used	Trial Number	Time (seconds)	Distance (centimeters)	Average Velocity (cm/s)
0	1			
0	2			
2	1			
2	2			
Length of Inflated Balloon (cm)				

Analyze and Conclude

1. **Applying Concepts** Use Newton's second and third laws to explain the motion of the balloon jet.

   _____

   _____

2. **Analyzing Data** How did adding mass (nuts) to the balloon jet affect its motion?

   _____

   _____

Exploration Lab

Determining Buoyant Force

In this lab, you will analyze recorded data to determine the buoyant forces acting on objects.

Problem

How does the buoyant force determine whether an object sinks?

Materials

- LabPro interface
- Logger *Pro* software
- Vernier dual-range force sensor
- string
- rock
- can
- plastic tub
- sponge
- paper towels
- 100-g standard mass
- wooden block tied to a fishing weight
- 250-mL graduated cylinder

Skills

Measuring, Calculating

Procedure 🔒 🔁

1. Record your trial results in the data table.
2. Connect the dual-range force sensor into Channel 1 of the LabPro interface. Set the switch on the front of the sensor to the lowest setting (± 10 N).
3. Launch Logger *Pro* and open the Buoyant Force.xmbl file. Logger *Pro* will display the force measurement in a meter on the computer screen.
4. With nothing suspended from the force sensor, click [Zero] to zero the sensor.

5. Tie one end of the string around the rock. Tie the other end to the hook on the force sensor. Suspend the rock from the sensor and measure and record its weight in air in your data table.

6. Place the can in an upright position in the plastic tub. Completely fill the can with water. Wipe up any water that has spilled into the tub. **CAUTION** *Wipe up any water that spills on the floor to avoid slips and falls.*

7. Lower the rock into the water until it is completely submerged. Some of the water may spill from the can into the tub. In your data table, record the apparent weight in water of the submerged rock. Remove the rock from the can.

8. Without spilling any water, carefully remove the can from the tub. Pour the water from the tub into the graduated cylinder. Record the volume of displaced water in your data table.

9. Repeat Steps 5 through 8, first with the 100-g standard mass and then with the wooden block that is tied to a fishing weight.

10. To determine the buoyant force on each object, subtract its apparent weight in water from its weight in air. Record these values.

11. Calculate the weight of the water each object displaces. (*Hint:* 1.0 mL of water has a weight of 0.0098 N.) Record these weights.

**Vernier
Lab 5**

Data Table

Object	Weight in Air (N)	Apparent Weight in Water (N)	Buoyant Force (weight in air — apparent weight in water, N)	Volume of Displaced Water (mL)	Weight of Displaced Water (N)
Rock					
100-g standard mass					
Wood block with fishing weight					

Analyze and Conclude

1. Observing What force is responsible for the difference between the weight of each object in the air and its apparent weight in water?

_____

_____

2. Analyzing Data How is the buoyant force related to the weight of water displaced?

_____

_____

3. Forming Operational Definitions Define buoyant force and describe two ways you can measure it or calculate it.

_____

_____

_____

4. Drawing Conclusions Explain what causes an object to sink or to float, using the terms *buoyancy, weight, force, density,* and *gravity.*

_____

_____

_____

Application Lab

Investigating a Spring Clip

There are many ways to use potential energy. A spring clip is a device used to hold weights on a barbell. The spring clip stores energy when you compress it. In this lab, you will determine how the distance you compress a spring clip is related to the force you apply and to the spring's potential energy.

Problem

How does the force you apply to a spring clip affect its elastic potential energy?

Materials

- LabPro interface
- Logger *Pro* software
- Vernier dual-range force sensor
- clamp
- spring clip
- heavy twine
- metric ruler
- graph paper

Skills

Measuring, Using Tables and Graphs

Procedure 🖉 🖾

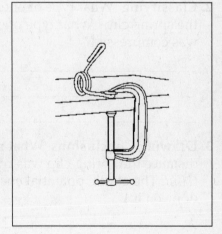

1. Using the clamp, firmly attach one handle of the spring clip to a tabletop, with the other handle facing up and away from the table as shown. **CAUTION** *Be careful not to pinch your fingers with the clamp or spring clip.*

2. Connect the dual-range force sensor into Channel 1 of the LabPro interface. Set the switch on the front of the sensor to the highest setting (± 50 N).

3. Launch Logger *Pro* and open the Spring Clip.xmbl file. Logger *Pro* will display the force measurement in a meter on the computer screen.

4. With nothing suspended from the force sensor, click ⌐ Zero ⌐ to zero the sensor.

5. Tie the hook of the force sensor to the upper handle of the spring clip using heavy twine. Have a classmate hold a metric ruler next to the spring clip as shown. Read the height of the upper handle of the spring clip. Record the measurement in the data table at the end of the lab. Have your teacher check your setup for safety before you proceed any further.

6. Slowly pull the force sensor down at a right angle to the upper handle until the handle moves about 0.1 cm. Record the force displayed on the computer screen and the height of the upper handle. Slowly release the force sensor.

7. Repeat step 6, this time pulling the handle 0.2 cm from the starting position.

8. Continue to repeat step 6, pulling the handle 0.1 cm farther each time. Continue to pull on the handle until the force sensor reaches its maximum force or you cannot squeeze the spring clip any farther. You may need to add more rows to the end of your data table for recording handle position and force.

9. Graph your data. Place the total distance the handle moved on the horizontal axis and the force applied on the vertical axis.

Analyze and Conclude

1. **Using Graphs** What is the approximate relationship between the total distance you compressed the spring clip and the force you applied to it?

_____

_____

_____

2. **Classifying** What type of energy transfer did you use to compress the spring clip? What type of energy did the spring clip gain when it was compressed?

_____

_____

_____

3. **Drawing Conclusions** What relationship exists between the distance the spring clip was compressed and its potential energy? (*Hint:* The elastic potential energy of the spring equals the work done on it.)

_____

_____

Data Table

Total Distance Moved (cm)	Position of Handle (cm)	Force (N)
0.0 cm		
0.1 cm		
0.2 cm		
0.3 cm		
0.4 cm		
0.5 cm		
0.6 cm		
0.7 cm		
0.8 cm		
0.9 cm		
1.0 cm		
1.1 cm		
1.2 cm		
1.3 cm		
1.4 cm		
1.5 cm		
1.6 cm		
1.7 cm		
1.8 cm		
1.9 cm		
2.0 cm		
2.1 cm		
2.2 cm		
2.3 cm		
2.4 cm		
2.5 cm		

Design Your Own Lab

Using Specific Heat to Analyze Metals

In this lab, you will determine the specific heat of steel and of aluminum. Then you will use specific heat to analyze the composition of a metal can.

Problem

How can you use specific heat to determine the composition of a metal can?

Materials

- LabPro interface
- Logger *Pro* software
- Vernier stainless steel temperature probe
- 10 steel bolts
- balance
- 50-cm length of string
- clamp
- ring stand
- boiling water bath
- 500-mL graduated cylinder
- ice water
- foam cup with lid
- aluminum nails
- crushed can

Skills

Calculating, Designing Experiments

Procedure 🌀 🏠 🔦 ⚗️

Part A: Determining Specific Heat

1. Record your measurements in the data table at the end of the lab.

2. Connect the stainless steel temperature probe into Channel 1 of the LabPro.

3. Launch Logger *Pro* and open the Specific Heat-Metals.xmbl file.

4. Logger *Pro* will display the temperature measurement in a meter on the computer screen. If the probe is in air, verify that it reads the correct room temperature.

5. Measure and record the mass of 10 steel bolts.

6. Tie all 10 bolts to one end of the
   string. Use a clamp and ring stand
   to suspend the bolts in the boiling
   water bath. **CAUTION** *Be careful
   not to splash boiling water.* After a
   few minutes, record the water
   temperature as the initial
   temperature of the bolts.

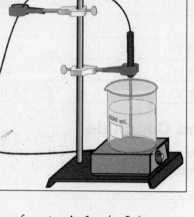

7. Remove the temperature probe
   from the water bath and allow it
   to cool to room temperature.

8. Use a graduated cylinder to pour
   200 mL of ice water (without ice)
   into the foam cup. Record the
   mass of the ice water. (*Hint:* The density of water is 1 g/mL.)

9. Use the clamp to move the bolts into the cup of ice water.
   Cover the cup and insert the temperature probe through the
   hole in the cover.

10. Gently swirl the water in the cup. Record the highest temperature
    as the final temperature for both the water and the steel bolts.

11. Calculate and record the specific heat of steel. (*Hint:* Use
    the equation $Q = m \times c \times \Delta T$ to calculate the energy the
    water absorbs.)

12. Repeat Steps 5 through 11 with aluminum nails to determine the
    specific heat of aluminum. Start by making a new data table.
    Use a mass of aluminum that is close to the mass you used for
    the steel bolts.

Part B: Design Your Own Experiment

13. **Designing Experiments** Design an experiment that uses specific
    heat to identify the metals a can might be made of.

14. Construct a data table in which to record your observations. After
    your teacher approves your plan, perform your experiment.

**Vernier
Lab 7**

Data Table

Measurement	Water	Steel Bolt
Mass (g)		
Initial temperature (°C)		
Final temperature (°C)		
Specific heat (J/g·°C)	4.18	

Analyze and Conclude

1. **Comparing and Contrasting** Which metal has a higher specific heat, aluminum or steel?

_____

_____

2. **Drawing Conclusions** Was the specific heat of the can closer to the specific heat of steel or of aluminum? What can you conclude about the material in the can?

_____

_____

3. **Evaluating** Did your observations prove what the can was made of? If not, what other information would you need to be sure?

_____

_____

_____

4. **Inferring** The can you used is often called a tin can. The specific heat of tin is 0.23 J/g·°C. Did your data support the idea that the can was made mostly of tin? Explain your answer.

_____

_____

_____

Forensics Lab

Evaluating Electrical Safety

Electrical appliances must be safely insulated to protect users from injury. In this lab, you will play the role of a safety engineer determining whether an electric power supply is safely insulated.

Problem

How much resistance is needed in series with a known resistance to reduce the voltage by 99 percent?

Materials

- LabPro interface
- Logger *Pro* software
- Vernier voltage probe
- 9-volt battery
- battery clip
- 3 alligator clips
- 4 resistors: 1 ohm, 10 ohms, 100 ohms, 1000 ohms

Skills

Calculating, Using Tables

Procedure 🔲 🔋 🔏 🔧

1. Use the data table at the end of the lab to record your voltage readings.
2. Connect the voltage probe into Channel 1 of the LabPro.
3. Launch Logger *Pro* and open the Electrical Safety.xmbl file.
4. Logger *Pro* will display the voltage measurement in a meter on the computer screen.

5. Attach the battery clip to the battery.
   CAUTION *The circuit may become hot.*

6. Use an alligator clip to attach one wire of the
   1-ohm resistor to one of the battery clip's wires
   as shown.

7. Clip one wire of the 1000-ohm resistor to the
   free end of the 1-ohm resistor. Clip the other
   wire of the 1000-ohm resistor to the free wire of
   the battery clip.

8. The 1-ohm resistor represents the current-
   carrying part of the appliance. The 1000-ohm
   resistor represents the insulation for the current-carrying part.
   Attach one of the voltage probe's leads to each wire of the 1-ohm
   resistor. Record the displayed voltage in your data table.

9. Attach one of the voltage probe's leads to each wire of the 1000-
   ohm resistor. Record the displayed voltage in your data table.

10. To model a reduction in the resistance of the insulation, repeat
    Steps 7 through 9, replacing the 1000-ohm resistor with the
    100-ohm resistor. Disconnect the resistors from the battery clip.

11. **Predicting** Record your prediction of how increasing the
    resistance of the current-carrying part of an appliance will affect
    the voltage difference across the insulating part.

12. To test your prediction, repeat Steps 6 through 10, using
    the 10-ohm resistor to represent the current-carrying part
    of the appliance.

Data Table

Current-Carrying Resistance (ohms)	Insulating Resistance (ohms)	Current-Carrying Voltage Difference (volts)	Insulating Voltage Difference (volts)
1	1000		
1	100		
10	1000		
10	100		

Analyze and Conclude

1. **Calculating** When the resistance of the current-carrying part was 1 ohm and the resistance of the insulating part was 100 ohms, what was the ratio of the voltage differences across the current-carrying part and the insulating part?

_____

_____

2. **Drawing Conclusions** In the circuit you built, what is the voltage difference across each resistor proportional to?

_____

_____

3. **Applying Concepts** If you know the resistance of the current-carrying part of an appliance, what should the resistance of the insulation be to reduce the voltage by 99 percent?

_____

_____

Application Lab

Investigating an Electric Generator

All generators have two main parts—a magnet and a wire that is wrapped into many coils. Usually, one of these parts remains in place as the other moves. The arrangement of these parts varies, depending on the size and power of the generator and whether it produces direct or alternating current. In this lab, you will determine how several variables affect the current produced by a simple generator.

Problem

How do the direction in which the magnet moves and the number and direction of the wire coil windings affect the current that a generator produces?

Materials

- LabPro interface
- Logger *Pro* software
- Vernier current probe
- 5-m insulated wire
- cardboard tube
- bar magnet
- graph paper
- metric ruler

Skills

Observing, Using Graphs

Procedure 🔲 ✂

Part A: Changing the Number of Coils

1. Slip the insulated wire between your hand and the cardboard tube so that 15 cm of wire extends from the tube. Use your other hand to wrap the long end of the wire around the tube 10 times in a clockwise direction near the top of the tube. Make sure all the coils are within 10 cm of the end of the tube. **CAUTION** *Be careful not to cut yourself on the sharp ends of the wire.*

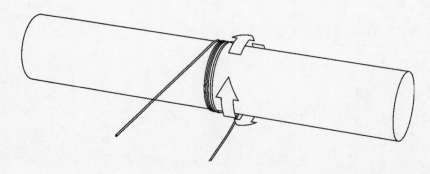

2. Secure the cardboard tube in place using a ring stand or have a fellow student hold the tube in place. Position something soft below the tube to catch the bar magnet when it is dropped.

3. Connect the red terminal on the current probe to the end of the insulated wire that is closer to the coils. Connect the black terminal on the current probe to the end of the wire that is farther from the coils. Connect the current probe into Channel 1 of the LabPro interface.

4. Launch Logger *Pro* and open the Electric Generator.xmbl file. Logger *Pro* will display the current (A) measurement in a meter on the computer screen.

5. Click ⬜ Zero ⬜ to adjust the measurements of the current probe to read a current of zero amps.

6. Hold the cardboard tube vertically with the red terminal at the bottom of the coil. Hold the bar magnet by its south pole and insert it into the tube to the point at which the center of the bar magnet is in line with the coiled wire.

7. Click on ⬜▶Collect⬜ to begin data collection on the computer. As soon as data collection begins, release the bar magnet so that it drops through the tube.

8. Click on the Statistics button to calculate the maximum current measured during data collection. Record in the data table at the end of the lab the maximum current displayed in the statistics box that appears on the computer screen.

Statistics Button

9. Disconnect the end of the wire that is connected to the black terminal of the current probe.

10. **Predicting** Record your prediction of how increasing the number of wire coils will affect the current.

11. To test your prediction, wrap the wire around the tube 10 more times in the same direction that you wound it previously—clockwise. You should now have a total of 20 coils. Reconnect the wire to the black terminal of the current probe.

12. Repeat Steps 6 through 8.

13. Again, disconnect the current probe from the black terminal. Wrap the wire clockwise around the tube 10 more times for a total of 30 coils. Reconnect the wire to the probe.

14. Repeat Steps 6 through 8.

Part B: Changing Other Properties of the Generator

15. **Predicting** Record your prediction of how reversing the direction of the magnet will affect the current.

16. To test your prediction, repeat Steps 6 through 8, but this time hold the magnet by its north pole.

17. **Predicting** Record your prediction of how reversing the direction of the wire coils will affect the current if you hold the magnet by its south pole.

18. To test your prediction, disconnect the current probe from the wire. Unwind the wire coils. Rewind the wire around the tube 30 times, holding the tube and the wire as you did in Step 1, but winding the wire in the opposite direction—counterclockwise. Reconnect the red terminal to the insulated wire extending from the bottom of the coil. Reconnect the black terminal to the wire extending from the top of the coil.

19. Repeat Steps 6 through 8.

20. Construct a graph using the data from the first three rows in your data table. Plot the number of coils on the horizontal axis and the current on the vertical axis.

Data Tables

Number of Coils	Direction of Coils	Pole Inserted	Current (A)
10	Clockwise	North	
20	Clockwise	North	
30	Clockwise	North	
30	Clockwise	South	
30	Counterclockwise	North	

Prediction 1	
Prediction 2	
Prediction 3	

Analyze and Conclude

1. Inferring What caused the current to flow in the wire?

_____

_____

2. Using Graphs Based on your graph, what is the relationship between the number of coils and the amount of current?

_____

_____

3. Analyzing Data Explain the effect that reversing the direction of the magnet or the coils had on the direction of the current.

_____

_____

4. Predicting Explain whether a generator could be built with a stationary magnet and wire coils that moved.

_____

_____

_____

5. Evaluating and Revising Did your observations support your predictions? If not, evaluate any flaws in the reasoning you used to make the predictions.

_____

_____

_____

Exploration Lab

Determining Relative Humidity

To measure relative humidity, you can use two temperature sensors. An absorbent wick keeps the bulb of one temperature sensor wet. When air flows over the wet bulb, the rate of evaporation increases. In this lab, you will discover how two temperature sensors measure the relative humidity of the surrounding air.

Problem

How can you measure relative humidity?

Materials

- LabPro interface
- Logger *Pro* software
- 2 Vernier stainless steel temperature probes
- piece of shoelace, 5 cm long
- masking tape

Skills

Using Tables, Formulating Hypotheses

Procedure 🐢 👤 🔌 ✋ 🖐

1. Connect the first stainless steel temperature probe into Channel 1 of the LabPro interface. Connect the second temperature probe into Channel 2 of the LabPro interface.

2. Launch Logger *Pro* and open the Relative Humidity.xmbl file.

3. Logger *Pro* will display the temperature measurement in a meter on the computer screen. If the probes are in air, verify that each reads the room temperature.

4. Slip probe 2 into a 5-cm piece of shoelace until the probe tip is at the middle of the shoelace piece. Fasten the shoelace to the probe with masking tape.

5. Determine the dry-probe and wet-probe temperatures at site 1 (the classroom).

   a. Wet the shoelace on probe 2 by placing it into a beaker of water that is at or above room temperature. Probe 1 is to stay dry.

   b. Take a probe in each hand and gently wave the probes in the air.

   c. Continue waving the probes until the temperature values displayed on the calculator screen stop changing.

   d. Record both final temperatures in the data table at the end of the lab.

   e. Calculate the difference between your dry-bulb and wet-bulb temperatures.

   f. In the relative humidity chart at the end of the lab, find the row that lists the dry-bulb temperature that you recorded. Then find the column that lists the difference in temperature that you calculated. The number located where this row and column meet is the relative humidity of the classroom. Record the relative humidity in your data table.

6. Place the temperature probes on a flat surface. Observe the temperature of the wet-bulb probe every 30 seconds until it remains constant. Then, repeat Step 5 at a different location indicated by your teacher.

Vernier Lab 10

Relative Humidity Chart

To find the relative humidity, measure the wet-bulb and dry-bulb temperatures with a sling psychrometer. Find the dry-bulb reading in the left column and the difference between readings at the top of the table. The number where these readings intersect is the relative humidity in percent.

Relative Humidity (percent)													
Dry-Bulb Reading (°C)	Difference Between Wet-Bulb and Dry-Bulb Readings (°C)												
	1	2	3	4	5	6	7	8	9	10	11	12	13	14
5	86	72	58	45	33	20	7							
6	86	73	60	48	35	24	11							
7	87	74	62	50	38	26	15							
8	87	75	63	51	40	29	19	8						
9	88	76	64	53	42	32	22	12						
10	88	77	66	55	44	34	24	15	6					
11	89	78	67	56	46	36	27	18	9					
12	89	78	68	58	48	39	29	21	12					
13	89	79	69	59	50	41	32	23	15	7				
14	90	79	70	60	51	42	34	26	18	10				
15	90	80	71	61	53	44	36	27	20	13	6			
16	90	81	71	63	54	46	38	30	23	15	8			
17	90	81	72	64	55	47	40	32	25	18	11			
18	91	82	73	65	57	49	41	34	27	20	14	7		
19	91	82	74	65	58	50	43	36	29	22	16	10		
20	91	83	74	66	59	51	44	37	31	24	18	12	6	
21	91	83	75	67	60	53	46	39	32	26	20	14	9	
22	92	83	76	68	61	54	47	40	34	28	22	17	11	6
23	92	84	76	69	62	55	48	42	36	30	24	19	13	8
24	92	84	77	69	62	56	49	43	37	31	26	20	15	10
25	92	84	77	70	63	57	50	44	39	33	28	22	17	12
26	92	85	78	71	64	58	51	46	40	34	29	24	19	14
27	92	85	78	71	65	58	52	47	41	36	31	26	21	16
28	93	85	78	72	65	59	53	48	42	37	32	27	22	18
29	93	86	79	72	66	60	54	49	43	38	33	28	24	19
30	93	86	79	73	67	61	55	50	44	39	35	30	25	21

Data Table

Location	Dry-Bulb Temp. (°C)	Wet-Bulb Temp. (°C)	Relative Humidity From Chart (%)
Classroom			

Analyze and Conclude

1. **Analyzing Data** Why did the two temperature sensors have different temperatures?

   _____

   _____

   _____

   _____

2. **Formulating Hypotheses** Explain how the relative humidity of the air affected the difference between the temperatures of the two temperature sensors.

   _____

   _____

   _____

   _____

3. **Drawing Conclusions** What do you think caused the difference in relative humidity between the two locations?

   _____

   _____

4. **Predicting** How would the relative humidity change if you cooled the air in the classroom?

   _____

   _____

   _____

Go Further

Measure and record the temperature and relative humidity outside your school or at home at various times of the day for several days. Graph these data and explain any patterns that you observe.

Contents

Texas Instruments Lab

1. Investigating Changes in Temperature During Heating of Solids — Exploration Lab, p. 92 — 80
2. Predicting the Density of an Element — Exploration Lab, p. 150 — 83
3. Preparing a Salt by Neutralization — Exploration Lab, p. 254 — 87
4. Investigating a Balloon Jet — Exploration Lab, p. 383 — 91
5. Determining Buoyant Force — Exploration Lab, p. 405 — 94
6. Investigating a Spring Clip — Application Lab, p. 467 — 97
7. Using Specific Heat to Analyze Metals — Design Your Own Lab, p. 493 — 100
8. Evaluating Electrical Safety — Forensics Lab, p. 623 — 103
9. Investigating an Electric Generator — Application Lab, p. 648 — 106
10. Determining Relative Humidity — Exploration Lab, p. 783 — 110

Teacher Notes and Answers

Texas Instrument Labs — 123

Exploration Lab

Investigating Changes in Temperature During Heating of Solids

Lauric acid is a solid that is found in coconuts and processed foods that are made with coconut oil. Lauric acid is also used to make some soaps and cosmetics. In this lab, you will measure the temperature of ice and of lauric acid as these solids are heated and melt. You will graph the data you collect and compare the heating curves for ice and for lauric acid.

Problem

What happens to the temperature of a substance during a phase change?

Materials

- LabPro or CBL 2 interface
- TI graphing calculator
- DataMate program
- Vernier stainless steel temperature probe
- 500-mL beaker
- crushed ice
- hot plate
- clock with second hand
- test tube of lauric acid with a Vernier stainless steel temperature probe
- glass stirring rod
- graph paper

Skills

Measuring, Using Graphs

Procedure 🔥 🧤 🥽 🧪 ☣

Part A: Heating Ice

1. Use the data table found at the end of the lab to record your data. You may need to add more rows to the end of your data table if the solids do not melt within 20 minutes.
2. Connect the stainless steel temperature probe into Channel 1 of the LabPro or CBL 2 interface. Use the link cable to connect the TI graphing calculator to the interface. Firmly press in the cable ends.
3. Turn on the calculator and start the DATAMATE program. Press CLEAR to reset the program.
4. DataMate will automatically recognize the sensor and display the temperature measurement in the upper right corner of the calculator screen. If the probe is in air, verify that it reads the correct room temperature.

5. Fill a 500-mL beaker halfway with crushed ice. **CAUTION** *Use care when handling glassware to avoid breakage. Wipe up any spilled ice right away to avoid slips and falls.*

6. Place the beaker on a hot plate. Don't turn the hot plate on yet. Insert the stainless steel temperature probe into the ice. Because it takes several seconds for the probe to adjust to the temperature of its surroundings, wait 20 seconds and then measure the temperature of the ice. Record this temperature next to the 0 minutes entry in your data table.

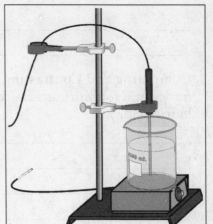

7. Turn the hot plate to a low setting. **CAUTION** *Be careful not to touch the hot plate because it could burn you.*

8. Observe and record the temperature of the water at one-minute intervals until all the ice has changed to liquid water. Circle the temperature at which you first observe liquid water and the temperature at which all the ice has changed to liquid water.

9. After all the ice has melted, make five more measurements of the temperature at one-minute intervals. Turn off the hot plate.

10. Graph your data with time on the horizontal axis and temperature on the vertical axis.

Part B: Heating Lauric Acid

11. Empty the water from the beaker into the sink. Fill the beaker halfway with cool tap water.

12. Place a test tube containing lauric acid and the stainless steel temperature probe into the beaker. If necessary, add or remove water from the beaker so that the surface of the water is above the surface of the lauric acid but below the opening of the test tube.

13. Place the beaker on the hot plate. After 20 seconds, measure the temperature of the lauric acid. Record this temperature next to the 0 minutes entry in your data table.

14. Repeat Steps 7 through 10 using the lauric acid instead of the ice. To keep the temperature the same throughout the water bath, use the glass stirring rod to stir the water after you take each temperature measurement.

Analyze and Conclude

1. **Using Graphs** Describe the shape of your graph for ice.

_____

_____

2. Analyzing Data What happened to the temperature of the ice-water mixture during the phase change?

_____

_____

_____

3. Comparing and Contrasting Compare the shapes of the graphs for ice and for lauric acid. Compare the melting points of ice and lauric acid.

_____

_____

_____

_____

Data Table

Time (minutes)	Temperature of Water (°C)	Temperature of Lauric Acid (°C)
0		
1		
2		
3		
4		
5		
6		
7		
8		
9		
10		
11		
12		
13		
14		
15		
16		
17		
18		
19		
20		

Exploration Lab

Predicting the Density of an Element

Density is a useful property for identifying and classifying elements.
In this lab, you will determine the densities of three elements in
Group 4A—silicon, tin, and lead. Then you will use your data to
predict the density of another element in Group 4A—germanium.

Problem

Can the densities of elements within a group be used to accurately
predict the density of another element in the group?

Materials

- LabPro or CBL 2 interface
- TI graphing calculator
- DataMate program
- Vernier dual-range force sensor
- unlined white paper
- scissors
- metric ruler
- yogurt cup with string
- forceps
- silicon
- tin
- lead shot
- 50-mL graduated cylinder
- graph paper
- periodic table

Skills

Measuring, Observing, Using Graphs, Calculating

Procedure 🥽 🧤 🔬 ✋ ✂️

Part A: Measuring Mass

1. Cut out three 10-cm × 10-cm pieces of paper from a sheet of
   unlined white paper. Label one piece of paper Silicon, the second
   Tin, and the third Lead.

2. Attach the force sensor to a ring stand so that the metal hook on the
   sensor is pointing toward the floor. Suspend the yogurt cup from
   the force sensor using the string attached to the cup.

3. Connect the dual-range force sensor into Channel 1 of the LabPro or CBL 2 interface. Set the switch on the front of the sensor to the lowest setting ($\pm$ 10 N). Use the link cable to connect the TI graphing calculator to the interface. Firmly press in the cable ends.

4. Turn on the calculator and start the DATAMATE program. Press CLEAR to reset the program.

5. DataMate will automatically recognize the sensor and display the force measurement in the upper right corner of the calculator screen. To zero the force readings from the sensor, follow the instructions below.

   ■ Select SETUP from the main screen.

   ■ Select ZERO from the setup screen.

   ■ Select CH1-FORCE(N) from the Select Channel menu.

   ■ With the empty cup suspended from the force sensor, press ENTER to zero the sensor.

6. Monitoring the measurements displayed on the calculator screen, pour enough silicon into the cup to reach a force of approximately 0.2 N. Divide the measurement displayed on the calculator screen by 0.0098 to calculate the mass of the silicon in grams. Record the mass in the data table at the end of the lab.

7. Empty the silicon from the cup onto the paper labeled Silicon.

8. Repeat Steps 6 and 7 for both tin and lead.

Part B: Measuring Volume

9. Place 25 mL of water in the graduated cylinder. Measure the volume of the water to the nearest 0.1 mL. Record the volume (in cm^3) in the data table at the end of the lab. (*Hint:* 1 mL = 1 cm^3)

10. Tilt the graduated cylinder and carefully pour the silicon from the paper into the graduated cylinder. Make sure that the silicon is completely covered by the water. Measure and record the volume of the water and silicon in your data table. Then, subtract the volume of water from the volume of the water and silicon. Record the result in your data table.

11. Repeat Steps 9 and 10 to find the volumes of tin and lead.

Part C: Calculating Density

12. To calculate the density of silicon, divide its mass by its volume.

$$\text{Density} = \frac{\text{Mass}}{\text{Volume}}$$

    Record the density of silicon in your data table.

13. Repeat Step 12 to find the densities of tin and lead.

14. Make a line graph that shows the relationship between the densities of silicon, tin, and lead and the periods in which they are located in the periodic table. Place the number of the period (from 1 to 7) on the horizontal axis and the density (in g/cm^3) on the vertical axis. Draw a straight line that comes as close as possible to all three points.

15. Germanium is in Period 4. To estimate the density of germanium, draw a dotted vertical line from the 4 on the horizontal axis to the solid line. Then, draw a dotted horizontal line from the solid line to the vertical axis. Read and record the density of germanium.

16. Wash your hands with warm water and soap before you leave the laboratory.

Data Table

Element	Mass of Element (g)	Volume of Water (cm³)	Volume of Water and Element (cm³)	Volume of Element (cm³)	Density of Element (g/cm³)
Silicon					
Tin					
Lead					

Analyze and Conclude

1. Classifying List lead, silicon, and tin in order of increasing density.

_____

_____

2. Comparing and Contrasting How does your estimate of the density of germanium compare with the actual density of germanium, which is 5.3 g/cm³?

_____

_____

3. Calculating Use the formula for percent error (PE) to calculate a percent error for your estimate of the density of germanium.

$$PE = \frac{\text{Estimated value} - \text{Accepted value}}{\text{Accepted value}} * 100$$

4. Drawing Conclusions How does the density of the elements change from silicon to lead in Group 4A?

_____

_____

Go Further

Use reference books or sites on the Internet to research properties of Group 4A elements. Construct a graph that shows how another property, such as melting point or boiling point, varies among the Group 4A elements you explored. Determine whether knowing the values for three of the elements would allow you to accurately predict a value for the fourth element.

Exploration Lab

Preparing a Salt by Neutralization

In this lab, you will prepare table salt by reacting hydrochloric acid (HCl) with sodium hydroxide (NaOH). To be sure that all of the acid and base have reacted, you will use phenolphthalein. You will first have to test the colors of this indicator with a known acid and base. After the acid and base have reacted, you will measure the pH of the solution with a pH sensor. Finally, you will evaporate the water and collect the sodium chloride.

Problem

How can you produce a salt by neutralization?

Materials

- LabPro or CBL 2 interface
- TI graphing calculator
- DataMate program
- Vernier pH sensor
- 3 dropper pipets
- labels
- 10-mL graduated cylinder
- test tube rack
- 2 10-mL test tubes
- distilled water
- hydrochloric acid
- sodium hydroxide solution
- 3 stirring rods
- phenolphthalein solution
- 2 25-mL beakers
- large watch glass
- 100-mL beaker
- hot plate

Skills

Observing, Measuring, Analyzing Data

Procedure 🐌 🗄 ⚠ 🔌 🧤

Part A: Preparing for the Experiment

1. Connect the pH sensor into Channel 1 of the LabPro or CBL 2 interface. Use the link cable to connect the TI graphing calculator to the interface. Firmly press in the cable ends.

2. Turn on the calculator and start the DATAMATE program. Press CLEAR to reset the program.

3. DataMate will automatically recognize the sensor and display the pH measurement in the upper right corner of the calculator screen.

4. Place about 10 mL of distilled water in a 25-mL beaker. Set the graduated cylinder on the table and add distilled water to the 5-mL mark. Be sure that the *bottom* of the meniscus is on the 5-mL line.

5. To determine the number of drops in 1.0 mL, use a clean dropper pipet to add 1 mL of water to the graduated cylinder. Hold the dropper pipet straight up and down with the tip of the dropper pipet just inside the mouth of the cylinder. As your partner watches the liquid level in the cylinder, add drops of water one at a time while counting the drops. Continue adding drops until the liquid level reaches 6 mL. Record the number of drops in 1 mL in the data table at the end of the lab.

6. Label one clean dropper pipet *Hydrochloric acid (HCl)* and the other *Sodium hydroxide (NaOH)*.

7. Using the HCl dropper pipet, add 3.0 mL of hydrochloric acid to a clean test tube. **CAUTION** *Hydrochloric acid is corrosive. In case of spills, wash thoroughly with water.* Add 2 to 3 drops of phenolphthalein to the test tube. Use a clean stirring rod to mix the hydrochloric acid and indicator. Record your observations.

8. Using the dropper pipet labeled NaOH, add 3.0 mL of sodium hydroxide solution to a clean test tube. **CAUTION** *Sodium hydroxide is corrosive. In case of spills, wash thoroughly with water.* Add 2 to 3 drops of phenolphthalein to the test tube. Use a clean stirring rod to mix the sodium hydroxide solution and indicator. Record your observations.

Part B: Making the Salt

9. Using the HCl dropper pipet, add 4.0 mL of hydrochloric acid to a clean 25-mL beaker. Record the number of drops you used. Add 2 to 4 drops of phenolphthalein to the beaker.

10. Use the NaOH dropper pipet to add sodium hydroxide drop by drop to the beaker of hydrochloric acid and phenolphthalein, stirring constantly. Count the drops as you add them. As a pink color remains longer, add the drops more slowly.

11. Continue to add and count the drops of sodium hydroxide until a
    light pink color remains for at least 30 seconds. (*Note:* If you add
    too much sodium hydroxide, add a few more drops of
    hydrochloric acid until the color disappears. Record any additional
    drops of hydrochloric acid that you added.) Then, carefully add
    sodium hydroxide until one drop produces a lasting pink color.
    Record the total number of drops of sodium hydroxide used.

12. Use the pH sensor to determine
    the pH of the final solution (the
    glass bulb at the tip of the probe
    must be submerged). Record the
    pH. If the pH is higher than 7.0,
    add hydrochloric acid drop by
    drop until the pH is equal to 7.0.
    Record the pH and the total
    number of drops of HCl
    you added.

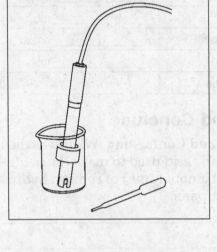

13. Pour the solution from the beaker
    into the watch glass.

14. Fill the 100-mL beaker about half
    full of water. Place the beaker on
    top of the hot plate.

15. Set the watch glass on top of the beaker.

16. Turn on the hot plate to a low setting. Adjust the heat as the water
    in the beaker warms. The water should simmer, but not boil.
    CAUTION *Do not touch the hot plate or the beaker.* Heat until a solid
    is visible at the edges of the water in the watch glass and the water
    is nearly evaporated. Turn off the heat.

17. Allow the remaining water to evaporate. Observe the contents of
    the watch glass. Record your observations.

18. When the watch glass has cooled, dispose of the contents as
    directed by your teacher. Clean up your equipment. Wash your
    hands with soap and water.

**Texas Instruments
Lab 3**

Data Table

Material(s)	Observation
1 ml	_____ drops
HCl + phenolphthalein	_____ (color)
NaOH + phenolphthalein	_____ (color)
Drops of HCl used	_____ drops
mL of HCl used	_____ mL
Drops of NaOH used	_____ drops
mL of NaOH used	_____ mL
pH of final solution	

Analyze and Conclude

1. **Comparing and Contrasting** What was the total amount (mL) of hydrochloric acid used to make the neutral solution? What was the total amount (mL) of sodium hydroxide? How do the amounts compare?

_____

_____

_____

2. **Drawing Conclusions** What do you conclude about the concentrations of hydrochloric acid and sodium hydroxide in the solutions?

_____

_____

3. **Predicting** If the acid had been twice as concentrated as the base, how would your data have changed?

_____

_____

Name _____ Class _____ Date _____

Exploration Lab

Investigating a Balloon Jet

In this lab, you will examine the relationships among force, mass, and motion.

Problem

How does a jet-powered device move?

Materials

- LabPro or CBL 2 interface
- TI graphing calculator
- DataMate program
- Vernier motion detector
- string, 3 m in length
- drinking straw
- 4 long balloons
- masking tape
- meter stick
- 2 threaded nuts
- 2 chairs

Skills

Applying Concepts

Procedure 📷

1. Connect the motion detector into the DIG/SONIC 1 port of the LabPro or CBL 2 interface. Use the link cable to connect the TI graphing calculator to the interface. Firmly press in the cable ends.

2. Turn on the calculator and start the DATAMATE program. Press CLEAR to reset the program.

3. DataMate will automatically recognize the sensor and display the distance measurement in the upper right corner of the calculator screen.

4. Insert the string through the straw and tie each end of the string to the back of a separate chair. Pull the chairs apart until the string is tight and horizontal.

5. Blow up the balloon and then hold the balloon's opening closed. Record the length of the balloon in the data table at the end of the lab. Have a classmate attach the balloon lengthwise to the straw using tape.

6. While continuing to hold the balloon's opening closed, have your classmate position the balloon jet so that the balloon's opening is 0.5 meters from a chair.

7. Hold up the motion detector next to the chair, aimed at the balloon and in line with the string. When the balloon is released, it should move away from the motion detector.

8. Select START to begin collecting data, and release the balloon.

9. After data collection stops, select DIG-DISTANCE and press [ENTER]. Use [►] to examine the data points along the graph. As you move the cursor right and left, the time (X) and distance (Y) values of each data point are displayed below the graph. Move the cursor to the point that marks the starting movement of the balloon. Note the distance and time. Round to the nearest 0.01 m. Move the cursor to the point that marks when the balloon stopped moving and note the final distance and time.

10. Calculate the total distance traveled by the balloon in the trial by subtracting the starting distance from the final distance. Calculate the total time by subtracting the starting time from the final time. Record your results in the data table for 0 Nuts Used, Trial 1.

11. Press [ENTER] to leave the graph screen. Select MAIN SCREEN to return to the main screen.

12. Repeat Steps 5 through 11 with a new balloon. Make sure to inflate the balloon to the same size as in Step 5. Record your results in the data table for 0 Nuts Used, Trial 2.

13. Repeat Steps 5 through 11 twice more with new balloons. This time, tape two nuts to the each balloon before releasing it. Record your results in the data table for 2 Nuts Used, Trials 1 and 2.

14. Calculate and record the average velocity for each trial. The average velocity is equal to the distance divided by the time.

Data Table

Number of Nuts Used	Trial Number	Time (seconds)	Distance (centimeters)	Average Velocity (cm/s)
0	1			
0	2			
2	1			
2	2			
Length of Inflated Balloon (cm)				

Analyze and Conclude

1. Applying Concepts Use Newton's second and third laws to explain the motion of the balloon jet.

_____

_____

2. Analyzing Data How did adding mass (nuts) to the balloon jet affect its motion?

_____

_____

Exploration Lab

Determining Buoyant Force

In this lab, you will analyze recorded data to determine the buoyant forces acting on objects.

Problem

How does the buoyant force determine whether an object sinks?

Materials

- LabPro or CBL 2 interface
- TI graphing calculator
- DataMate program
- Vernier dual-range force sensor
- string
- rock
- can
- plastic tub
- sponge
- paper towels
- 100-g standard mass
- wooden block tied to a fishing weight
- 250-mL graduated cylinder

Skills

Measuring, Calculating

Procedure 📖 🖉

1. Record your trial results in the data table.
2. Connect the dual-range force sensor into Channel 1 of the LabPro or CBL 2 interface. Set the switch on the front of the sensor to the lowest setting (± 10 N). Use the link cable to connect the TI graphing calculator to the interface. Firmly press in the cable ends.
3. Turn on the calculator and start the DATAMATE program. Press CLEAR to reset the program.
4. DataMate will automatically recognize the sensor and display the force measurement in the upper right corner of the calculator screen. To zero the force readings from the sensor, follow the instructions below.

   - Select SETUP from the main screen.
   - Select ZERO from the setup screen.
   - Select CH1-FORCE(N) from the Select Channel menu.
   - With nothing suspended from the force sensor, press ENTER to zero the sensor.

5. Tie one end of the string around the rock. Tie the other end to the hook on the force sensor. Suspend the rock from the sensor and measure and record its weight in air in your data table.

6. Place the can in an upright position in the plastic tub. Completely fill the can with water. Wipe up any water that has spilled into the tub. **CAUTION** *Wipe up any water that spills on the floor to avoid slips and falls.*

7. Lower the rock into the water until it is completely submerged. Some of the water may spill from the can into the tub. In your data table, record the apparent weight in water of the submerged rock. Remove the rock from the can.

8. Without spilling any water, carefully remove the can from the tub. Pour the water from the tub into the graduated cylinder. Record the volume of displaced water in your data table.

9. Repeat Steps 5 through 8, first with the 100-g standard mass and then with the wooden block that is tied to a fishing weight.

10. To determine the buoyant force on each object, subtract its apparent weight in water from its weight in air. Record these values.

11. Calculate the weight of the water each object displaces. (*Hint:* 1.0 mL of water has a weight of 0.0098 N.) Record these weights.

Data Table

Object	Weight in Air (N)	Apparent Weight in Water (N)	Buoyant Force (weight in air — apparent weight in water, N)	Volume of Displaced Water (mL)	Weight of Displaced Water (N)
Rock					
100-g standard mass					
Wood block with fishing weight					

Analyze and Conclude

1. **Observing** What force is responsible for the difference between the weight of each object in the air and its apparent weight in water?

_____

_____

2. **Analyzing Data** How is the buoyant force related to the weight of water displaced?

_____

_____

3. **Forming Operational Definitions** Define buoyant force and describe two ways you can measure it or calculate it.

_____

_____

_____

4. **Drawing Conclusions** Explain what causes an object to sink or to float, using the terms *buoyancy*, *weight*, *force*, *density*, and *gravity*.

_____

_____

_____

Application Lab

Investigating a Spring Clip

There are many ways to use potential energy. A spring clip is a device used to hold weights on a barbell. The spring clip stores energy when you compress it. In this lab, you will determine how the distance you compress a spring clip is related to the force you apply and to the spring's potential energy.

Problem

How does the force you apply to a spring clip affect its elastic potential energy?

Materials

- LabPro or CBL 2 interface
- DataMate program
- TI graphing calculator
- Vernier dual-range force sensor
- clamp
- spring clip
- heavy twine
- metric ruler
- graph paper

Skills

Measuring, Using Tables and Graphs

Procedure 🔲 🔲

1. Using the clamp, firmly attach one handle of the spring clip to a tabletop, with the other handle facing up and away from the table as shown. **CAUTION** *Be careful not to pinch your fingers with the clamp or spring clip.*

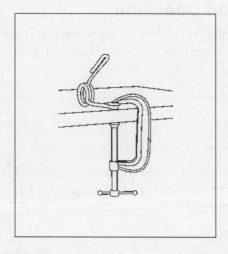

2. Connect the dual-range force sensor into Channel 1 of the LabPro or CBL 2 interface. Set the switch on the front of the sensor to the highest setting (± 50 N). Use the link cable to connect the TI graphing calculator to the interface. Firmly press in the cable ends.

3. Turn on the calculator and start the DATAMATE program. Press CLEAR to reset the program.

4. DataMate will automatically recognize the sensor and display the force measurement in the upper right corner of the calculator screen. To zero the force readings from the sensor, follow the instructions below.

   ▪ Select SETUP from the main screen.

   ▪ Select ZERO from the setup screen.

   ▪ Select CH1-FORCE(N) from the Select Channel menu.

   ▪ With nothing suspended from the force sensor, press ENTER to zero the sensor.

5. Tie the hook of the force sensor to the upper handle of the spring clip using heavy twine. Have a classmate hold a metric ruler next to the spring clip. Read the height of the upper handle of the spring clip. Record the measurement in the data table at the end of the lab. Have your teacher check your setup for safety before you proceed any further.

6. Slowly pull the force sensor down at a right angle to the upper handle until the handle moves about 0.1 cm. Record the force displayed on the calculator screen and the height of the upper handle. Slowly release the force sensor.

7. Repeat step 6, this time pulling the handle 0.2 cm from the starting position.

8. Continue to repeat step 6, pulling the handle 0.1 cm farther each time. Continue to pull on the handle until the force sensor reaches its maximum force or you cannot squeeze the spring clip any farther. You may need to add more rows to the end of your data table for recording handle position and force.

9. Graph your data. Place the distance the handle moved on the horizontal axis and the maximum force applied on the vertical axis.

Analyze and Conclude

1. **Using Graphs** What is the approximate relationship between the total distance you compressed the spring clip and the force you applied to it?

_____

_____

_____

2. **Classifying** What type of energy transfer did you use to compress the spring clip? What type of energy did the spring clip gain when it was compressed?

_____

_____

_____

3. Drawing Conclusions What relationship exists between the
distance the spring clip was compressed and its potential energy?
(*Hint:* The elastic potential energy of the spring equals the work
done on it.)

_____

_____

Data Table

Total Distance Moved (cm)	Position of Handle (cm)	Force (N)
0.0 cm		
0.1 cm		
0.2 cm		
0.3 cm		
0.4 cm		
0.5 cm		
0.6 cm		
0.7 cm		
0.8 cm		
0.9 cm		
1.0 cm		
1.1 cm		
1.2 cm		
1.3 cm		
1.4 cm		
1.5 cm		
1.6 cm		
1.7 cm		
1.8 cm		
1.9 cm		
2.0 cm		
2.1 cm		
2.2 cm		
2.3 cm		
2.4 cm		
2.5 cm		

Texas Instruments
Lab 6

Design Your Own Lab

Using Specific Heat to Analyze Metals

In this lab, you will determine the specific heat of steel and of aluminum. Then you will use specific heat to analyze the composition of a metal can.

Problem

How can you use specific heat to determine the composition of a metal can?

Materials

- LabPro or CBL 2 interface
- TI graphing calculator
- DataMate program
- Vernier stainless steel temperature probe
- 10 steel bolts
- balance
- 50-cm length of string
- clamp
- ring stand
- boiling water bath
- 500-mL graduated cylinder
- ice water
- foam cup with lid
- aluminum nails
- crushed can

Skills

Calculating, Designing Experiments

Procedure 🌀 🔧 🔩 ⚖

Part A: Determining Specific Heat

1. Record your measurements in the data table at the end of the lab.
2. Connect the stainless steel temperature probe into Channel 1 of the LabPro or CBL 2 interface. Use the link cable to connect the TI graphing calculator to the interface. Firmly press in the cable ends.
3. Turn on the calculator and start the DATAMATE program. Press [CLEAR] to reset the program.

4. DataMate will automatically recognize the sensor and display the temperature measurement in the upper right corner of the calculator screen. If the probe is in air, verify that it reads the correct room temperature.

5. Measure and record the mass of 10 steel bolts.

6. Tie all 10 bolts to the string. Use a clamp and ring stand to suspend the bolts in the boiling water bath. **CAUTION** *Be careful not to splash boiling water.* After a few minutes, record the water temperature as the initial temperature of the bolts.

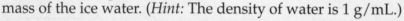

7. Remove the temperature probe from the water bath and allow it to cool to room temperature.

8. Use a graduated cylinder to pour 200 mL of ice water (without ice) into the foam cup. Record the mass of the ice water. (*Hint:* The density of water is 1 g/mL.)

9. Use the clamp to move the bolts into the cup of ice water. Cover the cup and insert the temperature probe through the hole in the cover.

10. Gently swirl the water in the cup. Record the highest temperature as the final temperature for both the water and the steel bolts.

11. Calculate and record the specific heat of steel. (*Hint:* Use the equation $Q = m \times c \times \Delta T$ to calculate the energy the water absorbs.)

12. Repeat Steps 5 through 11 with aluminum nails to determine the specific heat of aluminum. Start by making a new data table. Use a mass of aluminum that is close to the mass you used for the steel bolts.

Part B: Design Your Own Experiment

13. **Designing Experiments** Design an experiment that uses specific heat to identify the metals a can might be made of.

14. Construct a data table in which to record your observations. After your teacher approves your plan, perform your experiment.

Data Table

Measurement	Water	Steel Bolt
Mass (g)		
Initial temperature (°C)		
Final temperature (°C)		
Specific heat (J/g·°C)	4.18	

Analyze and Conclude

1. **Comparing and Contrasting** Which metal has a higher specific heat, aluminum or steel?

   _____

   _____

2. **Drawing Conclusions** Was the specific heat of the can closer to the specific heat of steel or of aluminum? What can you conclude about the material in the can?

   _____

   _____

3. **Evaluating** Did your observations prove what the can was made of? If not, what other information would you need to be sure?

   _____

   _____

   _____

4. **Inferring** The can you used is often called a tin can. The specific heat of tin is 0.23 J/g·°C. Did your data support the idea that the can was made mostly of tin? Explain your answer.

   _____

   _____

   _____

Chapter 20

Lab 8

Forensics Lab

Evaluating Electrical Safety

Electrical appliances must be safely insulated to protect users from injury. In this lab, you will play the role of a safety engineer determining whether an electric power supply is safely insulated.

Problem

How much resistance is needed in series with a known resistance to reduce the voltage by 99 percent?

Materials

- LabPro or CBL 2 interface
- TI graphing calculator
- DataMate program
- Vernier voltage probe
- 9-volt battery
- battery clip
- 3 alligator clips
- 4 resistors: 1 ohm, 10 ohms, 100 ohms, 1000 ohms

Skills

Calculating, Using Tables

Procedure 🐢 🔧 🗂 🔨

1. Use the data table at the end of the lab to record your voltage
2. Connect the voltage probe into Channel 1 of the LabPro or CBL 2 interface. Use the link cable to connect the TI graphing calculator to the interface. Firmly press in the cable ends.
3. Turn on the calculator and start the DATAMATE program. Press CLEAR to reset the program.
4. DataMate will automatically recognize the sensor and display the voltage measurement in the upper right corner of the calculator screen.

5. Attach the battery clip to the battery. **CAUTION** *The circuit may become hot.*

6. Use an alligator clip to attach one wire of the 1-ohm resistor to one of the battery clip's wires as shown.

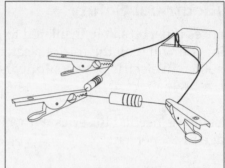

7. Clip one wire of the 1000-ohm resistor to the free end of the 1-ohm resistor. Clip the other wire of the 1000-ohm resistor to the free wire of the battery clip.

8. The 1-ohm resistor represents the current-carrying part of an appliance. The 1000-ohm resistor represents the insulation for the current-carrying part. Attach one of the voltage probe's leads to each wire of the 1-ohm resistor. Record the displayed voltage in your data table.

9. Attach one of the voltage probe's leads to each wire of the 1000-ohm resistor. Record the displayed voltage in your data table.

10. To model a reduction in the resistance of the insulation, repeat Steps 7 through 9, replacing the 1000-ohm resistor with the 100-ohm resistor. Disconnect the resistors from the battery clip.

11. **Predicting** Record your prediction of how increasing the resistance of the current-carrying part of an appliance will affect the voltage difference across the insulating part.

12. To test your prediction, repeat Steps 6 through 10, using the 10-ohm resistor to represent the current-carrying part of the appliance.

Data Table

Current-Carrying Resistance (ohms)	Insulating Resistance (ohms)	Current-Carrying Voltage Difference (volts)	Insulating Voltage Difference (volts)
1	1000		
1	100		
10	1000		
10	100		

Analyze and Conclude

1. **Calculating** When the resistance of the current-carrying part was 1 ohm and the resistance of the insulating part was 100 ohms, what was the ratio of the voltage differences across the current-carrying part and the insulating part?

_____

_____

2. **Drawing Conclusions** In the circuit you built, what is the voltage difference across each resistor proportional to?

_____

_____

3. **Applying Concepts** If you know the resistance of the current-carrying part of an appliance, what should the resistance of the insulation be to reduce the voltage by 99 percent?

_____

_____

Texas Instruments
Lab 8

Application Lab

Investigating an Electric Generator

All generators have two main parts—a magnet and a wire that is wrapped into many coils. Usually one of these parts remains in place as the other moves. The arrangement of these parts varies, depending on the size and power of the generator and whether it produces direct or alternating current. In this lab, you will determine how several variables affect the current produced by a simple generator.

Problem

How do the direction in which the magnet moves and the number and direction of the wire coil windings affect the current that a generator produces?

Materials

- LabPro or CBL 2 interface
- TI graphing calculator
- DataMate program
- Vernier current probe
- 5-m insulated wire
- cardboard tube
- bar magnet
- graph paper
- metric ruler

Skills

Observing, Using Graphs

Procedure 🗒 🔧

Part A: Changing the Number of Coils

1. Slip the insulated wire between your hand and the tube so that 15 cm of wire extends from the tube. Use your other hand to wrap the long end of the wire around the tube 10 times in a clockwise direction near the top of the tube. Make sure that all of the coils are within 10 cm of the end of the tube. **CAUTION** *Be careful not to cut yourself on the sharp ends of the wire.*

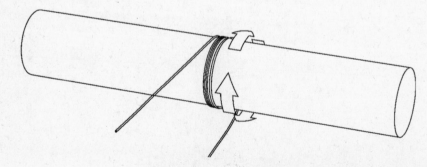

2. Secure the cardboard tube in place using a ring stand or have a fellow student hold the tube in place. Position something soft below the tube to catch the bar magnet when it is dropped.

3. Connect the red terminal on the current probe to the end of the wire that is closer to the coils. Connect the black terminal on the current probe to the end of the wire that is farther from the coils. Connect the current probe into Channel 1 of the LabPro or CBL 2 interface. Use the link cable to connect the TI graphing calculator to the interface. Firmly press in the cable ends.

4. Turn on the calculator and start the DATAMATE program. Press CLEAR to reset the program.

5. DataMate will automatically recognize the sensor and display the current (A) measurement in the upper right corner of the calculator screen. To zero the readings from the sensor, follow the instructions below.

   ▪ Select Setup from the main screen.

   ▪ Select ZERO from the setup screen.

   ▪ Select CH1-CURRENT(A) from the Select Channel menu.

   ▪ Press ENTER to adjust the measurements of the current probe to read a current of zero amps.

6. Hold the cardboard tube vertically with the red terminal at the bottom of the coil. Hold the bar magnet by its south pole and insert it into the tube to the point at which the center of the bar magnet is in line with the coiled wire.

7. Select START to begin data collection on the calculator. As soon as data collection begins, release the bar magnet so that it drops through the tube.

8. When data collection has finished, a graph of CURRENT *vs.* TIME will be displayed. Press ► repeatedly to move the blinking trace cursor from data point to data point on the graph. Move the cursor until it rests on the peak of the current graph. The current measurement in amps will be displayed as a Y-value at the bottom of the calculator screen. Record the peak current in the data table at the end of the lab. Press ENTER to return to the main screen.

9. Disconnect the end of the wire that is connected to the black terminal of the current probe.

10. **Predicting** Record your prediction of how increasing the number of wire coils will affect the current.

11. To test your prediction, wrap the wire around the tube 10 more times in the same direction that you wound it previously— clockwise. You should now have a total of 20 coils. Reconnect the wire to the black terminal of the current probe.

12. Repeat Steps 6 through 8.

13. Again, disconnect the current probe from the black terminal. Wrap the wire clockwise around the cardboard tube 10 more times for a total of 30 coils. Reconnect the wire to the probe.

14. Repeat Steps 6 through 8.

Part B: Changing Other Properties of the Generator

15. **Predicting** Record your prediction of how reversing the direction of the magnet will affect the current.

16. To test your prediction, repeat Steps 6 through 8, but this time hold the magnet by its north pole.

17. **Predicting** Record your prediction of how reversing the direction of the wire coils will affect the current.

18. To test your prediction, disconnect the current probe from the wire. Unwind the wire coils. Rewind the wire around the tube 30 times, holding the tube and the wire as you did in step 1, but winding the wire in the opposite direction—counterclockwise. Reconnect the red terminal to the insulated wire extending from the bottom of the coils. Reconnect the black terminal to the wire extending from the top of the coils.

19. Repeat Steps 6 through 8.

20. Construct a graph using the data from the first three rows of your data table. Plot the number of coils on the horizontal axis and the current on the vertical axis.

Data Tables

Number of Coils	Direction of Coils	Pole Inserted	Current (A)
10	Clockwise	North	
20	Clockwise	North	
30	Clockwise	North	
30	Clockwise	South	
30	Counterclockwise	North	

Prediction 1	
Prediction 2	
Prediction 3	

Analyze and Conclude

1. Inferring What caused the current to flow in the wire?

_____

_____

2. Using Graphs Based on your graph, what is the relationship between the number of coils and the amount of current?

_____

_____

3. Analyzing Data Explain the effect that reversing the direction of the magnet or the coils had on the direction of the current.

_____

_____

4. Predicting Explain whether a generator could be built with a stationary magnet and wire coils that moved.

_____

_____

_____

5. Evaluating and Revising Did your observations support your predictions? If not, evaluate any flaws in the reasoning you used to make the predictions.

_____

_____

_____

Texas Instruments Lab 9

Exploration Lab

Determining Relative Humidity

To measure relative humidity, you can use two temperature sensors. An absorbent wick keeps the bulb of one temperature sensor wet. When air flows over the wet bulb, the rate of evaporation increases. In this lab, you will discover how two temperature sensors measure the relative humidity of the surrounding air.

Problem

How can you measure relative humidity?

Materials

- LabPro or CBL 2 interface
- TI graphing calculator
- DataMate program
- 2 Vernier stainless steel temperature probes
- piece of shoelace, 5 cm long
- masking tape

Skills

Using Tables, Formulating Hypotheses

Procedure 🤿 🧤 🔦 ☝ 🔥

1. Connect the first stainless steel temperature probe into Channel 1 of the LabPro or CBL 2 interface. Connect the second temperature probe into Channel 2 of the LabPro or CBL 2 interface. Use the link cable to connect the TI graphing calculator to the interface. Firmly press in the cable ends.

2. Turn on the calculator and start the DATAMATE program. Press [CLEAR] to reset the program.

3. DataMate will automatically recognize the sensors and display the temperature measurements in the upper right corner of the calculator screen. If the probes are in air, verify that each reads the room temperature.

4. Slip probe 2 into a 5-cm piece of shoelace until the probe tip is at the middle of the shoelace piece. Fasten the shoelace to the probe with masking tape.

5. Determine the dry-probe and wet-probe temperatures at site 1 (the classroom).

   a. Wet the shoelace on probe 2 by placing it into a beaker of water that is at or above room temperature. Probe 1 is to stay dry.

   b. Take a probe in each hand and gently wave the probes in the air.

   c. Continue waving the probes until the temperature values displayed on the calculator screen stop changing.

   d. Record both final temperatures in the data table at the end of the lab.

   e. Calculate the difference between your dry-bulb and wet-bulb temperatures.

   f. In the relative humidity chart at the end of the lab, find the row that lists the dry-bulb temperature that you recorded. Then find the column that lists the difference in temperature that you calculated. The number located where this row and column meet is the relative humidity of the classroom. Record the relative humidity in your data table.

6. Place the temperature probes on a flat surface. Observe the temperature of the wet-bulb probe every 30 seconds until it remains constant. Then, repeat Step 5 at a different location indicated by your teacher.

Texas Instruments
Lab 10

Relative Humidity Chart

To find the relative humidity, measure the wet-bulb and dry-bulb temperatures with a sling psychrometer. Find the dry-bulb reading in the left column and the difference between readings at the top of the table. The number where these readings intersect is the relative humidity in percent.

Relative Humidity (percent)														
Dry-Bulb Reading (°C)	Difference Between Wet-Bulb and Dry-Bulb Readings (°C)													
	1	2	3	4	5	6	7	8	9	10	11	12	13	14
5	86	72	58	45	33	20	7							
6	86	73	60	48	35	24	11							
7	87	74	62	50	38	26	15							
8	87	75	63	51	40	29	19	8						
9	88	76	64	53	42	32	22	12						
10	88	77	66	55	44	34	24	15	6					
11	89	78	67	56	46	36	27	18	9					
12	89	78	68	58	48	39	29	21	12					
13	89	79	69	59	50	41	32	23	15	7				
14	90	79	70	60	51	42	34	26	18	10				
15	90	80	71	61	53	44	36	27	20	13	6			
16	90	81	71	63	54	46	38	30	23	15	8			
17	90	81	72	64	55	47	40	32	25	18	11			
18	91	82	73	65	57	49	41	34	27	20	14	7		
19	91	82	74	65	58	50	43	36	29	22	16	10		
20	91	83	74	66	59	51	44	37	31	24	18	12	6	
21	91	83	75	67	60	53	46	39	32	26	20	14	9	
22	92	83	76	68	61	54	47	40	34	28	22	17	11	6
23	92	84	76	69	62	55	48	42	36	30	24	19	13	8
24	92	84	77	69	62	56	49	43	37	31	26	20	15	10
25	92	84	77	70	63	57	50	44	39	33	28	22	17	12
26	92	85	78	71	64	58	51	46	40	34	29	24	19	14
27	92	85	78	71	65	58	52	47	41	36	31	26	21	16
28	93	85	78	72	65	59	53	48	42	37	32	27	22	18
29	93	86	79	72	66	60	54	49	43	38	33	28	24	19
30	93	86	79	73	67	61	55	50	44	39	35	30	25	21

Data Table

Location	Dry-Bulb Temp. (°C)	Wet-Bulb Temp. (°C)	Relative Humidity From Chart (%)
Classroom			

Analyze and Conclude

1. **Analyzing Data** Why did the two temperature sensors have different temperatures?

_____

_____

_____

2. **Formulating Hypotheses** Explain how the relative humidity of the air affected the difference between the temperatures of the two temperature sensors.

_____

_____

_____

3. **Drawing Conclusions** What do you think caused the difference in relative humidity between the two locations?

_____

_____

4. **Predicting** How would the relative humidity change if you cooled the air in the classroom?

_____

_____

_____

Go Further

Measure and record the temperature and relative humidity outside your school or at home at various times of the day for several days. Graph these data and explain any patterns that you observe.

Texas Instruments
Lab 10

Teacher Notes and Answers
PASCO Labs

Exploration Lab: Investigating Changes in Temperature During Heating of Solids

Objective

After completing this activity, students will be able to

- explain the relatively constant temperature of a substance that is undergoing a phase change.

Address Misconceptions

Students might think the temperature should keep increasing as ice melts. Ask them to predict the shape of the melting curve. After performing the lab, ask students to explain the shape of the curve.

Prep Time 30 minutes

Advance Prep

Buy crushed ice or crush it by placing ice cubes into a plastic bag and hitting them with a mallet. Pour granular lauric acid into the test tubes. If you have two temperature sensors for each student or lab group, insert a temperature probe in each test tube. After the first class has used these test tubes, the lauric acid will be melted. Rather than discarding the melted lauric acid, leave the temperature probes in the test tubes and allow the test tubes to cool to room temperature. The probes will be embedded in the solidified lauric acid.

Class Time 45 minutes

Safety

Hot plates should be positioned away from the edges of tables, and power cords should be placed safely behind the hot plates, where they are not likely to become accidentally entangled with arms or clothing. Once a hot plate is turned on, students should not touch it.

Teaching Tips

- Emphasize the importance of measuring the initial temperature of the ice as accurately as possible after inserting the temperature probe.
- You may wish to save time by having some students perform Part A of the lab and others perform Part B. Students can then exchange and graph their data.
- To help students construct their graphs, show a sample graph on an overhead transparency.

- You may wish to postpone the graphing of the results of Part A in Step 11 to the end of the lab, after all data have been collected.

Collecting Data Using the Xplorer

- For the best results in the laboratory, connect the Xplorer to the computer using a USB cable.
- Data can also be collected and stored in the Xplorer.
- To download data from the Xplorer to a computer, plug the Xplorer into your computer. At the DataStudio prompt, click Retrieve Now to transfer the collected data into DataStudio. Data automatically download to your computer and appear on the computer screen in a DataStudio display.

Expected Outcome

In Part A, if the readings are taken quickly enough, the first few temperature readings may be below 0°C. The temperature readings should remain at 0°C until all the ice has melted. The temperature should begin to rise once the ice has melted. Heating solid lauric acid raises its temperature to its melting point of approximately 45°C. The temperature will begin to rise again after the lauric acid has melted.

Sample Data

Ice melts at 0°C, and lauric acid melts at approximately 45°C.

Analyze and Conclude

1. The graph rises quickly to 0°C and remains horizontal at that temperature for several minutes. Then, it begins to rise again in a straight line.
2. The temperature remained constant until the phase change was completed.
3. The two graphs had similar shapes. However, ice melted at 0°C and lauric acid melted at approximately 45°C.

Exploration Lab: Predicting the Density of an Element

Objectives

After completing this activity, students will be able to

- state that density increases going down a group in the periodic table.
- evaluate as approximate predictions of physical properties based on the periodic table.

Prep Time 20 minutes

Advance Prep

Place each of the elements into a separate, small, labeled container. If 50-mL graduated cylinders are unavailable, you can use cylinders of a different size. However, the larger graduations on some larger cylinders will reduce the precision of measurements, and smaller cylinders may be too narrow to accommodate large samples.

Class Time 40 minutes

Safety

Make sure that students wear safety goggles, disposable plastic gloves, and lab aprons and wash their hands before leaving the laboratory. Caution students about the proper handling of chemicals. If you cut pieces of tin for students to use, be sure to file the edges smooth. Do not discard lead.

Teaching Tips

- Review the proper techniques for accurate measurement of volume in the graduated cylinder by reading from the bottom of the meniscus.

Sample Data

Questioning Strategies

Ask students, **Why is it necessary to subtract the volume of water from the total volume of water and sample when determining the volume of the silicon, tin, and lead?** *(To obtain the volume of each element.)*

Collecting Data Using the Xplorer

- For the best results in the laboratory, connect the Xplorer to the computer using a USB cable.
- Data can also be collected and stored in the Xplorer.
- To download data from the Xplorer to a computer, plug the Xplorer into your computer. At the DataStudio prompt, click Retrieve Now to transfer the collected data into DataStudio. Data automatically download to your computer and appear on the computer screen in a DataStudio display.

Expected Outcome

The densities of elements increase from the top to the bottom of Group 4A, but not in a simple linear manner.

Element	Mass of Element (g)	Volume of Water (mL)	Volume of Water and Element (mL)	Volume of Element (cm³)	Density (g/cm³)
Tin	22.14	25.0	28.0	3.0	7.38 g/cm³
Lead	21.31	25.0	27.0	2.0	10.66 g/cm³
Silicon	20.10	25.0	33.5	8.5	2.37 g/cm³

Analyze and Conclude

1. Silicon, tin, and lead
2. A typical student estimate for the density of germanium is 4.6 g/cm^3, which is a rough approximation of the actual value of 5.3 g/cm^3.
3. Student estimates are likely to be approximately 16% lower than the actual value.
4. The density of the elements increases from the top to the bottom of Group 4A, but not in a simple linear manner.

Go Further

Students will discover that there also is a relationship, though slight, between position in the periodic table and many other physical properties such as melting and boiling points.

Exploration Lab: Preparing a Salt by Neutralization

Objectives

After completing this activity, students will be able to

- perform a neutralization reaction.
- detect the occurrence of a neutralization reaction using an indicator.

Prep Time 20 minutes

Advance Prep

Prepare solutions of 1 *M* hydrochloric acid and 1 *M* sodium hydroxide. To help students keep track of their solutions, prepare sets of labeled test tubes for each group of students. Provide each group with about 8 mL of each solution.

Class Time 40 minutes

Safety

Students should use caution with the acid and base solutions. Hydrochloric acid and sodium hydroxide are corrosive. In case of spills, clean thoroughly with water. Caution students not to touch the hot plate or the heated beaker. Have students observe safety symbols and wear safety goggles, rubber gloves, and lab aprons.

Teaching Tips

- When determining the number of drops in a milliliter, one student should place the tip of the dropper inside the opening of the graduated cylinder and count the drops while a second student kneels to examine the graduated cylinder at eye level.
- Students should read the level of the graduated cylinder while it is sitting on a flat surface. Remind students to read the bottom of the meniscus when making volume measurements.
- Show students how to label the pipets.
- The size of the beaker used in Step 16 depends on the size of the evaporating dish. A small evaporating dish may require a smaller beaker.
- Show students the proper method for using a pH sensor and how to avoid contaminating samples by rinsing the probe properly. Be sure that students understand that the pH sensor must be stored in solution when not being used.
- Combine all waste solutions, and add acid or base until litmus or a pH sensor indicates neutrality. Dispose of the neutral solution in the sink with excess water.

Collecting Data Using the Xplorer

- For the best results in the laboratory, connect the Xplorer to the computer using a USB cable.
- Data can also be collected and stored in the Xplorer.
- To download data from the Xplorer to a computer, plug the Xplorer into your computer. At the DataStudio prompt, click Retrieve Now to transfer the collected data into DataStudio. Data automatically download to your computer and appear on the computer screen in a DataStudio display.

Expected Outcome

It will take approximately the same number of milliliters of each solution to reach neutralization.

Sample Data

Materials	Observations
1 mL	22 drops
HCl + phenolphthalein	Clear
NaOH + phenolphthalein	Pink
Drops of HCl used	88 drops
mL of HCl used	4 mL
Drops of NaOH used	88 drops
mL of NaOH used	4 mL
pH of final solution	7

Analyze and Conclude

1. It will take approximately the same number of milliliters of each solution to reach neutralization.
2. The concentrations are the same.
3. It would have taken half as much acid to reach the color change.

Exploration Lab: Investigating a Balloon Jet

Objective

After completing this activity, students will be able to

- use Newton's second and third laws of motion to explain the movement of a jet-powered device.
- use Newton's second and third laws of motion to describe how the mass of an object affects its acceleration in response to a force.

Address Misconceptions

Many students hold the misconception that a jet functions by pushing against the surrounding air. Point out that rockets work in airless outer space. Then ask students to explain how they think the balloon jet moves. As the air in the balloon jet escapes out the end it produces an equal and opposite reaction in the balloon, which accelerates the balloon forward.

Prep Time 10 minutes

Class Time 30 minutes

Teaching Tips

- Inform students that the path the balloon travels should be clear of all objects, or otherwise the motion detector will only measure the distance to the closest object.

Collecting Data Using the Xplorer

- For the best results in the laboratory, connect the Xplorer to the computer using a USB cable.
- Data can also be collected and stored in the Xplorer.
- To download data from the Xplorer to a computer, plug the Xplorer into your computer. At the DataStudio prompt, click Retrieve Now to transfer the collected data into DataStudio. Data automatically download to your computer and appear on the computer screen in a DataStudio display.

Expected Outcome

As the balloon is released it will accelerate along the length of the string. Adding to the mass of the balloon will reduce the time and distance that the balloon travels.

Sample Data

Number of Nuts Used	Trial Number	Average Velocity (cm/s)
0	1	−1.04
0	2	−1.02
2	3	−0.34
2	4	−0.57

Analyze and Conclude

1. A jet's movement depends on Newton's third law of motion. The pressurized air inside the sealed balloon pushes outward in all directions, but as long as the air can't go anywhere, neither can the balloon. As soon as the air inside the balloon is allowed to escape, the force of the air on the opened end of the balloon no longer balances the force of air on the opposite, closed end. This unbalanced force moves the balloon. Newton's second law of motion predicts that the balloon will accelerate at a rate that is directly proportional to the force of the compressed air, and inversely proportional to the balloon's mass.
2. Adding nuts increased the mass of the balloon jet, which reduced its acceleration.

Exploration Lab: Determining Buoyant Force

Objective

After completing this lab, students will be able to
- define the buoyant force as the difference between an object's weight in air and its apparent weight in water.
- state that the buoyant force on an object floating in water is equal to the weight of the water the object displaces.

Prep Time 10 minutes

Advance Prep

If possible, supply a standard mass with a hook for ease of weighing. Attach enough mass to the wooden block to ensure that it will exert a measurable force on the force sensor when the block is in water.

Class Time 30 minutes

Teaching Tips

- Ask students why it was necessary to attach a weight to the wooden block. Explain that the weight is necessary to ensure that the wooden block will exert a measurable force on the spring scale when the block is in water.
- Instruct students on the proper use and zeroing of a force sensor.

Collecting Data Using the Xplorer

- For the best results in the laboratory, connect the Xplorer to the computer using a USB cable.
- Data can also be collected and stored in the Xplorer.
- To download data from the Xplorer to a computer, plug the Xplorer into your computer. At the DataStudio prompt, click Retrieve Now to transfer the collected data into DataStudio. Data automatically download to your computer and appear on the computer screen in a DataStudio display.

Expected Outcome

The buoyant force on each object is equal to the weight of the water it displaces.

Sample Data

Object	Weight in Air (N)	Apparent Weight in Water (N)	Buoyant Force (weight in air — apparent weight in water, N)	Volume of Displaced Water (mL)	Weight of Displaced Water (N)
Rock	0.6 N	0.4 N	0.2 N	22 mL	0.2 N
100-g standard mass	1.0 N	0.8 N	0.2 N	12 mL	0.1 N
Wood block with fishing weight	1.7 N	0.2 N	1.5 N	184 mL	1.8 N

Analyze and Conclude

1. The difference is equal to the buoyant force that the water exerts on the object.
2. They are equal.
3. The buoyant force on an object is equal to the difference between its weight in air and its apparent weight in water. It is also equal to the weight of the water the object displaces.
4. An object will float when the upward force of buoyancy is greater than or equal to the downward force of gravity (the weight of the object). For the buoyant force to counteract the gravitational force, the object must weigh as much as or less than the volume of water it displaces. For this reason, floating objects have low densities.

Application Lab: Investigating a Spring Clip

Objective

After completing this activity, students will be able to

- describe the relationship between an applied force and the resulting change in elastic potential energy.

Skills Focus

Observing, Measuring, Using Tables and Graphs

Prep Time 10 minutes

Advance Prep

Spring clips can be purchased from department or sporting-goods stores. C-clamps can be purchased from hardware stores.

Class Time 40 minutes

Safety

Check students' setups in Step 6 to make sure that the spring clip is securely clamped to the table and will not come loose when compressed. The force sensor should be tied securely to the spring clip.

Teaching Tips

- Make sure that students do not exceed the limits of either the force sensor or the spring clip. If either is stretched too far, the instruments may not work properly in the future.
- Instruct students on the proper use and zeroing of a force sensor.

Collecting Data Using the Xplorer

- For the best results in the laboratory, connect the Xplorer to the computer using a USB cable.
- Data can also be collected and stored in the Xplorer.
- To download data from the Xplorer to a computer, plug the Xplorer into your computer. At the DataStudio prompt, click Retrieve Now to transfer the collected data into DataStudio. Data automatically download to your computer and appear on the computer screen in a DataStudio display.

Expected Outcome

There should be a linear relationship between force and distance. As distance increases, force increases.

Analyze and Conclude

1. As the distance increased, the force increased. The relationship between force and distance is directly proportional.
2. Kinetic energy was transformed into elastic potential energy when the spring clip was compressed. This action increased the elastic potential energy of the spring clip.
3. The greater the distance the exerciser was compressed, the greater its elastic potential energy.

Design Your Own Lab: Using Specific Heat to Analyze Metals

Objective
After completing this lab, students will be able to
- describe how specific heat is determined.

Address Misconceptions
Students may have the misconception that the temperatures of the metal and water are the only factors that will affect the final temperature of the mixture. To help dispel this misconception, ask them to compare the effects of dropping an ice cube into a lake and into a glass of water.

Prep Time 20 minutes

Advance Prep
Crush a steel can (commonly referred to as a "tin" can) for each lab group. Puncture the lids of the foam cups to enable students to insert the temperature probes. Smooth any rough or sharp edges with a file while wearing heavy leather gloves and safety goggles. Each student or group will need a boiling water bath and ring stand. Alternatively, a large beaker of boiling water on a hot plate can be provided for the entire class to use. Put a temperature probe in the beaker. Place one or more ring stands next to the boiling water bath. Students can attach their clamps to the ring stands to suspend the bolts in the boiling water. Cut 50-cm lengths of string for suspending the bolts in the boiling water bath.

Class Time 45 minutes

Safety
Remind students to be careful of boiling water. It may scald them. Use tongs or heat-resistant gloves when handling hot objects and hot liquids. Students should wear safety goggles and lab aprons and should not stir with the temperature probes. Keep all cords safely away from the surface of the hot plate.

Teaching Tips
- Students may need some guidance in using the specific heat equation.
- Show students how to place the lid over the string that extends out of the foam cup in Step 9.

Questioning Strategies
Ask students the following questions.

Why is it important to quickly transfer the bolts into the beaker? *(Because the bolts are very hot, they will lose thermal energy very quickly as soon as they leave the hot water.)*

Why is it important to swirl the water after adding the hot bolts? *(This ensures an even temperature and more accurate results.)*

Collecting Data Using the Xplorer
- For the best results in the laboratory, connect the Xplorer to the computer using a USB cable.
- Data can also be collected and stored in the Xplorer.
- To download data from the Xplorer to a computer, plug the Xplorer into your computer. At the DataStudio prompt, click Retrieve Now to transfer the collected data into DataStudio. Data automatically download to your computer and appear on the computer screen in a DataStudio display.

Expected Outcome
Students should measure a specific heat for the steel can that is close to that of the steel bolts.

Sample Data
Ten bolts with a mass of 100 g will raise the temperature of 200 mL of water by about 5°C. The same mass of aluminum nails will raise the temperature by about 9°C.

Answers to Analyze and Conclude
1. Aluminum has a higher specific heat than steel.
2. The specific heat of the can was very close to the specific heat of steel. This is evidence that the can is made mostly of steel.
3. The observations support the idea that the can is made of steel, but do not prove it; other metals may have similar heat capacities. A list of the heat capacities of various metals for comparison would be helpful, as would other kinds of evidence, such as the densities and chemical properties of the metals.
4. The specific heat of the can is close to that of steel, not tin. This suggests that the can is made of steel.

Forensics Lab: Evaluating Electrical Safety

Objective

After completing this activity, students will be able to

- determine the voltage differences across resistances in series.

Prep Time 20 minutes

Advance Preparation

Strip insulation from the ends of the wires attached to the battery clips. Label the resistors with their resistances. Each resistor has four colored bands at one end. From the end of the resistor inward, the first three bands for the resistors used in this lab are 1 ohm: brown, black, gold; 10 ohms: brown, black, black; 100 ohms: brown, black, brown; and 1000 ohms: brown, black, red. The fourth band indicates the accuracy of the labeled resistance.

Class Time 45 minutes

Safety

Caution students to be careful with the sharp tips of the wires when assembling the circuit, and when handling the circuits that are turned on. The circuit parts may become hot.

Collecting Data Using the Xplorer

- For the best results in the laboratory, connect the Xplorer to the computer using a USB cable.
- Data can also be collected and stored in the Xplorer.
- To download data from the Xplorer to a computer, plug the Xplorer into your computer. At the DataStudio prompt, click Retrieve Now to transfer the collected data into DataStudio. Data automatically download to your computer and appear on the computer screen in a DataStudio display.

Expected Outcome

The voltage difference across each resistor in the circuit is proportional to its resistance. The total voltage difference across both resistors is equal to the voltage of the battery, which may decline after the battery has been used.

Analyze and Conclude

1. The ratio of the voltage differences was 0.01 (1 : 100).
2. The voltage difference across each resistor was proportional to its resistance.
3. The resistance of the insulation should be 100 times the resistance of the current-carrying part.

Application Lab: Investigating an Electric Generator

Objective

After completing this activity, students will be able to

- describe how an electric generator works.

Prep Time 15 minutes

Advance Prep

Cut a 5-m length of wire for each group and strip 3 cm of the insulation from the ends of the wires. Provide cardboard tubes from empty bathroom paper rolls.

Class Time 45 minutes

Safety

Students should wear safety goggles and lab aprons.

Sample Data

Current-Carrying Resistance (ohms)	Insulating Resistance (ohms)	Current-Carrying Voltage Difference (volts)	Insulating Voltage Difference (volts)
1	1000	0.01	9.0
1	100	0.09	7.6
10	1000	0.09	8.9
10	100	0.82	7.9

Sample Data

Number of Coils	Direction of Coils	Pole Inserted	Current (mA)
10	Clockwise	North	0.0136
20	Clockwise	North	0.0268
30	Clockwise	North	0.0430
30	Counterclockwise	South	−0.0411
30	Clockwise	North	−0.0391

Teaching Tips

- In Step 24 and subsequent steps, make sure that students read the sign or direction of the current correctly. In Step 24, this information will be the reverse of the direction observed in the previous steps.
- Show students how to insert the bar magnet so that the center of the bar is in line with the coils. The magnet should always be released at the same point.
- When dropping the bar magnet through the coil, students should place something soft on the floor below to avoid damaging or disturbing the magnetic field of the magnets.

Collecting Data Using the Xplorer

- For the best results in the laboratory, connect the Xplorer to the computer using a USB cable.
- Data can also be collected and stored in the Xplorer.
- To download data from the Xplorer to a computer, plug the Xplorer into your computer. At the DataStudio prompt, click Retrieve Now to transfer the collected data into DataStudio. Data automatically download to your computer and appear on the computer screen in a DataStudio display.

Expected Outcome

The current is directly proportional to the number of coils. Reversing the poles of the magnet or the direction of the coils reverses the direction of the current.

Answers to Analyze and Conclude

1. A current flowed in the wire because the moving magnetic field exerted a force on the electrons in the wire, causing them to move.
2. The graph indicates a direct proportion between the number of coils and the current.
3. Reversing the direction of the magnet or the coils reversed the direction of the force of the magnetic field on the electrons in the wire. This change in direction caused the current to flow in the opposite direction.

4. It does not matter which part moves to accomplish this task. It is only necessary that the magnetic field in the wire coil change.
5. A correct prediction should state that reversing the direction of the magnet or the wire coils will reverse the direction of the current.

Exploration Lab: Determining Relative Humidity

Objective

After completing this activity, students will be able to
- explain how to determine relative humidity.

Address Misconceptions

Students may confuse relative humidity and absolute humidity. Explain that relative humidity is not an absolute measurement of the amount of moisture in the atmosphere. Point out to students that relative humidity is expressed as a percentage of the maximum possible absolute humidity at a particular temperature. A common misconception is that relative humidity is a percentage of the water-holding capacity of air. Unlike liquid solvents that have a finite ability to dissolve various solids, air does not have a temperature-dependent holding capacity for water vapor. Rather, 100% relative humidity describes a situation in which the water vapor in the air is in equilibrium with the vapor pressure above a surface of pure water. Many people believe incorrectly that humid air is denser than dry air. Use a periodic table to show students that the water molecule's molecular mass is substantially less than those of N_2 and O_2 that account for nearly all the mass of dry air.

Prep Time 15 minutes

Advance Prep

Make certain that the relative humidity charts that you supply to students express temperatures in degrees Celsius, to match the temperature probe measurements that students will use in the lab.

Class Time 40 minutes

Teaching Tips

- When recording measurements outside of the classroom, be sure that your Xplorer has fresh batteries.
- Designate a second location at which to record the relative humidity in Step 17. This site could be outdoors, the cafeteria, or a hallway.

Collecting Data Using the Xplorer

- For the best results in the laboratory, connect the Xplorer to the computer using a USB cable.
- Data can also be collected and stored in the Xplorer.
- To download data from the Xplorer to a computer, plug the Xplorer into your computer. At the DataStudio prompt, click Retrieve Now to transfer the collected data into DataStudio. Data automatically download to your computer and appear on the computer screen in a DataStudio display.

Expected Outcome

The wet-bulb temperature probe will have a lower temperature than the dry-bulb temperature probe.

Sample Data

Typical data could consist of a dry-bulb reading of 21°C, a wet-bulb reading of 15°C, and a relative humidity of 51%. Data will depend on local conditions. In any case, the wet-bulb reading will be less than or equal to the dry-bulb reading.

Analyze and Conclude

1. The temperature of the wet-bulb temperature probe is usually lower than the temperature of the dry-bulb temperature probe because evaporation of water from the wet bulb absorbed energy from the wet-bulb temperature probe, which cooled the temperature probe.

2. The difference in temperature between the two temperature probes depends on the degree to which evaporation cools the wet bulb. The lower the relative humidity, the greater is the rate at which water evaporates, cooling the wet bulb. Relative humidity does not affect the temperature of the dry-bulb temperature probe. Therefore, the lower the relative humidity, the cooler the wet bulb will be, and the greater the difference in temperature between the two temperature probes will be.

3. Factors that are likely to affect the relative humidity in various locations include sources of water, especially warm water, and variation in the effectiveness of heating and cooling throughout the school building.

4. Cooling the room would increase the relative humidity. The maximum concentration of water vapor in air is reduced at lower temperatures. Therefore, as the air in the room is cooled, the same concentration of water vapor becomes a higher percentage of the maximum concentration, or a higher relative humidity.

5. If the temperature sensors and humidity sensor are working correctly, there should be no difference in the relative humidity measured by the sensor and the relative humidity found with the temperature sensors and the chart.

Go Further

Relative humidity is typically highest in early morning due to evaporation of moisture condensed during the night. Students may observe additional patterns of change in relative humidity depending on location, current weather conditions, and the season.

Teacher Notes and Answers
Vernier and Texas Instruments Labs

Exploration Lab: Investigating Changes in Temperature During Heating of Solids

Objective
After completing this activity, students will be able to
- explain the relatively constant temperature of a substance that is undergoing a phase change.

Address Misconceptions
Students might think the temperature should keep increasing as ice melts. Ask them to predict the shape of the melting curve. After performing the lab, ask students to explain the shape of the curve.

Prep Time 30 minutes

Advance Prep
Buy crushed ice or crush it by placing ice cubes into a plastic bag and hitting them with a mallet. Pour granular lauric acid into the test tubes. If you have two temperature sensors for each student or lab group, insert a temperature probe in each test tube. After the first class has used these test tubes, the lauric acid will be melted. Rather than discarding the melted lauric acid, leave the temperature probes in the test tubes and allow the test tubes to cool to room temperature. The probes will be embedded in the solidified lauric acid.

Class Time 45 minutes

Safety
Hot plates should be positioned away from the edges of tables, and power cords should be placed safely behind the hot plates, where they are not likely to become accidentally entangled with arms or clothing. Once a hot plate is turned on, students should not touch it.

Teaching Tips
- Emphasize the importance of measuring the initial temperature of the ice as accurately as possible after inserting the temperature probe.
- You may wish to save time by having some students perform Part A of the lab and others perform Part B. Students can then exchange and graph their data.
- To help students construct their graphs, show a sample graph on an overhead transparency.

- You may wish to postpone the graphing of the results of Part A in Step 10 to the end of the lab, after all data have been collected.

Expected Outcome
In Part A, if the readings are taken quickly enough, the first few temperature readings may be below 0°C. The temperature readings should remain at 0°C until all the ice has melted. The temperature should begin to rise once the ice has melted. Heating solid lauric acid raises its temperature to its melting point of approximately 45°C. The temperature will begin to rise again after the lauric acid has melted.

Sample Data
Ice melts at 0°C, and lauric acid melts at approximately 45°C.

Analyze and Conclude
1. The graph rises quickly to 0°C and remains horizontal at that temperature for several minutes. Then, it begins to rise again in a straight line.
2. The temperature remained constant until the phase change was completed.
3. The two graphs had similar shapes. However, ice melted at 0°C and lauric acid melted at approximately 45°C.

Exploration Lab: Predicting the Density of an Element

Objectives
After completing this activity, students will be able to
- state that density increases going down a group in the periodic table.
- evaluate as approximate predictions of physical properties based on the periodic table.

Prep Time 20 minutes

Advance Prep
Place each of the elements into a separate, small, labeled container. If 50-mL graduated cylinders are unavailable, you can use cylinders of a different size. However, the larger graduations on some larger cylinders will reduce the precision of measurements, and smaller cylinders may be too narrow to accommodate large samples. In clean, dry yogurt cups, cut four small holes equidistant from one another near the opening of the cup. Tie string through the holes to allow students to suspend the cups from the hook on the force sensors.

Sample Data

Element	Mass of Element (g)	Volume of Water (mL)	Volume of Water and Element (mL)	Volume of Element (cm³)	Density (g/cm³)
Tin	22.14	25.0	28.0	3.0	7.38 g/cm³
Lead	21.31	25.0	27.0	2.0	10.66 g/cm³
Silicon	20.10	25.0	33.5	8.5	2.37 g/cm³

Class Time 40 minutes

Safety

Make sure that students wear safety goggles, disposable plastic gloves, and lab aprons and wash their hands before leaving the laboratory. Caution students about the proper handling of chemicals. If you cut pieces of tin for students to use, be sure to file the edges smooth. Do not discard lead.

Teaching Tips

- Review the proper techniques for accurate measurement of volume in the graduated cylinder by reading from the bottom of the meniscus.
- Review the proper technique for setting up and zeroing a force sensor.

Questioning Strategies

Ask students, **Why is it necessary to subtract the volume of water from the total volume of water and sample when determining the volume of the silicon, tin, and lead?** (*To obtain the volume of each element.*)

Expected Outcome

The densities of elements increase from the top to the bottom of Group 4A, but not in a simple linear manner.

Analyze and Conclude

1. Silicon, tin, and lead
2. A typical student estimate for the density of germanium is 4.6 g/cm³, which is a rough approximation of the actual value of 5.3 g/cm³.
3. Student estimates are likely to be approximately 16% lower than the actual value.

4. The density of the elements increases from the top to the bottom of Group 4A, but not in a simple linear manner.

Go Further

Students will discover that there also is a relationship, though slight, between position in the periodic table and many other physical properties such as melting and boiling points.

Exploration Lab: Preparing a Salt by Neutralization

Objectives

After completing this activity, students will be able to
- perform a neutralization reaction.
- detect the occurrence of a neutralization reaction using an indicator.

Prep Time 20 minutes

Advance Prep

Prepare solutions of 1 *M* hydrochloric acid and 1 *M* sodium hydroxide. To help students keep track of their solutions, prepare sets of labeled test tubes for each group of students. Provide each group with about 8 mL of each solution.

Class Time 40 minutes

Safety

Students should use caution with the acid and base solutions. Hydrochloric acid and sodium hydroxide are corrosive. In case of spills, clean thoroughly with water. Caution students not to touch the hot plate or the heated beaker. Have students observe safety symbols and wear safety goggles, rubber gloves, and lab aprons.

Teaching Tips

- When determining the number of drops in a milliliter, one student should place the tip of the dropper inside the opening of the graduated cylinder and count the drops while a second student kneels to examine the graduated cylinder at eye level.
- Students should read the level of the graduated cylinder while it is sitting on a flat surface. Remind students to read the bottom of the meniscus when making volume measurements.
- Show students how to label the pipets.
- The size of the beaker used in Step 14 depends on the size of the evaporating dish. A small evaporating dish may require a smaller beaker.
- Show students the proper method for using a pH sensor and how to avoid contaminating samples by rinsing the probe properly. Be sure that students understand that the pH sensor must be stored in solution when not being used.
- Combine all waste solutions, and add acid or base until litmus or a pH sensor indicates neutrality. Dispose of the neutral solution in the sink with excess water.

Expected Outcome

It will take approximately the same number of milliliters of each solution to reach neutralization.

Sample Data

Materials	Observations
1 mL	22 drops
HCl + phenolphthalein	Clear
NaOH + phenolphthalein	Pink
Drops of HCl used	88 drops
mL of HCl used	4 mL
Drops of NaOH used	88 drops
mL of NaOH used	4 mL
pH of final solution	7

Analyze and Conclude

1. It will take approximately the same number of milliliters of each solution to reach neutralization.
2. The concentrations are the same.
3. It would have taken half as much acid to reach the color change.

Exploration Lab: Investigating a Balloon Jet

Objective

After completing this activity, students will be able to

- use Newton's second and third laws of motion to explain the movement of a jet-powered device.
- use Newton's second and third laws of motion to describe how the mass of an object affects its acceleration in response to a force.

Address Misconceptions

Many students hold the misconception that a jet functions by pushing against the surrounding air. Point out that rockets work in airless outer space. Then ask students to explain how they think the balloon jet moves. As the air in the balloon jet escapes out the end it produces an equal and opposite reaction in the balloon, which accelerates the balloon forward.

Prep Time 10 minutes

Class Time 30 minutes

Teaching Tips

- Inform students that the path the balloon travels should be clear of all objects, or otherwise the motion detector will only measure the distance to the closest object.

Expected Outcome

As the balloon is released it will accelerate along the length of the string. Adding to the mass of the balloon will reduce the time and distance that the balloon travels.

Analyze and Conclude

1. A jet's movement depends on Newton's third law of motion. The pressurized air inside the sealed balloon pushes outward in all directions, but as long as the air can't go anywhere, neither can the balloon. As soon as the air inside the balloon is allowed to escape, the force of the air on the opened end of the balloon no longer balances the force of air on the opposite, closed end. This unbalanced force moves the balloon. Newton's second law of motion predicts that the balloon will accelerate at a rate that is directly proportional to the force of the compressed air, and inversely proportional to the balloon's mass.
2. Adding nuts increased the mass of the balloon jet, which reduced its acceleration.

Sample Data

Trial	Initial Time	Final Time	Time Traveled	Initial Distance	Final Distance	Distance Traveled	Average Velocity
Trial 1–0 nuts	0.59 s	0.83 s	0.24 s	0.47 m	2.96 m	2.49 m	10.38 m/s
Trial 2–0 nuts	0.51 s	0.79 s	0.28 s	0.47 m	2.89 m	2.42 m	8.64 m/s
Trial 1–2 nuts	0.65 s	1.08 s	0.43 s	0.47 m	0.93 m	0.46 m	1.07 m/s
Trial 2–2 nuts	0.59 s	1.06 s	0.47 s	0.47 m	0.89 m	0.42 m	0.89 m/s

Exploration Lab: Determining Buoyant Force

Objective
After completing this lab, students will be able to

- define the buoyant force as the difference between an object's weight in air and its apparent weight in water.
- state that the buoyant force on an object floating in water is equal to the weight of the water the object displaces.

Prep Time 10 minutes

Advance Prep
If possible, supply a standard mass with a hook for ease of weighing. Attach enough mass to the wooden block to ensure that it will exert a measurable force on the force sensor when the block is in water.

Class Time 30 minutes

Teaching Tips
- Ask students why it was necessary to attach a weight to the wooden block. Explain that the weight is necessary to ensure that the wooden block will exert a measurable force on the spring scale when the block is in water.
- Instruct students on the proper use and zeroing of a force sensor. Remind them that the switch on the front of the sensor should be set to ± 10 N.

Expected Outcome
The buoyant force on each object is equal to the weight of the water it displaces.

Analyze and Conclude
1. The difference is equal to the buoyant force that the water exerts on the object.
2. They are equal.
3. The buoyant force on an object is equal to the difference between its weight in air and its

Sample Data

Object	Weight in Air (N)	Apparent Weight in Water (N)	Buoyant Force (weight in air − apparent weight in water, N)	Volume of Displaced Water (mL)	Weight of Displaced Water (N)
Rock	0.6 N	0.4 N	0.2 N	22 mL	0.2 N
100-g standard mass	1.0 N	0.8 N	0.2 N	12 mL	0.1 N
Wood block with fishing weight	1.7 N	0.2 N	1.5 N	184 mL	1.8 N

apparent weight in water. It is also equal to the weight of the water the object displaces.

4. An object will float when the upward force of buoyancy is greater than or equal to the downward force of gravity (the weight of the object). For the buoyant force to counteract the gravitational force, the object must weigh as much as or less than the volume of water it displaces. For this reason, floating objects have low densities.

Application Lab: Investigating a Spring Clip

Objective
After completing this activity, students will be able to
- describe the relationship between an applied force and the resulting change in elastic potential energy.

Skills Focus
Observing, Measuring, Using Tables and Graphs

Prep Time 10 minutes

Advance Prep
Spring clips can be purchased from department or sporting-goods stores. C-clamps can be purchased from hardware stores.

Class Time 40 minutes

Safety
Check students' setups in Step 5 to make sure that the spring clip is securely clamped to the table and will not come loose when compressed. The force sensor should be tied securely to the spring clip.

Teaching Tips
- Make sure that students do not exceed the limits of either the force sensor or the spring clip. If either is stretched too far, the instruments may not work properly in the future.
- Instruct students on the proper use and zeroing of a force sensor. Remind them that the switch on the front of the sensor should be set to ± 50 N.

Expected Outcome
There should be a linear relationship between force and distance. As distance increases, force increases.

Analyze and Conclude
1. As the distance increased, the force increased. The relationship between force and distance is directly proportional.
2. Kinetic energy was transformed into elastic potential energy when the spring clip was

compressed. This action increased the elastic potential energy of the spring clip.
3. The greater the distance the exerciser was compressed, the greater its elastic potential energy.

Design Your Own Lab: Using Specific Heat to Analyze Metals

Objective
After completing this lab, students will be able to
- describe how specific heat is determined.

Address Misconceptions
Students may have the misconception that the temperatures of the metal and water are the only factors that will affect the final temperature of the mixture. To help dispel this misconception, ask them to compare the effects of dropping an ice cube into a lake and into a glass of water.

Prep Time 20 minutes

Advance Prep
Crush a steel can (commonly referred to as a "tin" can) for each lab group. Puncture the lids of the foam cups to enable students to insert the temperature probes. Smooth any rough or sharp edges with a file while wearing heavy leather gloves and safety goggles. Each student or group will need a boiling water bath and ring stand. Alternatively, a large beaker of boiling water on a hot plate can be provided for the entire class to use. Put a temperature probe in the beaker. Place one or more ring stands next to the boiling water bath. Students can attach their clamps to the ring stands to suspend the bolts in the boiling water. Cut 50-cm lengths of string for suspending the bolts in the boiling water bath.

Class Time 45 minutes

Safety
Remind students to be careful of boiling water. It may scald them. Use tongs or heat-resistant gloves when handling hot objects and hot liquids. Students should wear safety goggles and lab aprons and should not stir with the temperature probes. Keep all cords safely away from the surface of the hot plate.

Teaching Tips
- Students may need some guidance in using the specific heat equation.
- Show students how to place the lid over the string that extends out of the foam cup in Step 9.

Questioning Strategies

Ask students the following questions.

Why is it important to quickly transfer the bolts into the beaker? *(Because the bolts are very hot, they will lose thermal energy very quickly as soon as they leave the hot water.)*

Why is it important to swirl the water after adding the hot bolts? *(This ensures an even temperature and more accurate results.)*

Expected Outcome

Students should measure a specific heat for the steel can that is close to that of the steel bolts.

Sample Data

Ten bolts with a mass of 100 g will raise the temperature of 200 mL of water by about 5°C. The same mass of aluminum nails will raise the temperature by about 9°C.

Answers to Analyze and Conclude

1. Aluminum has a higher specific heat than steel.
2. The specific heat of the can was very close to the specific heat of steel. This is evidence that the can is made mostly of steel.
3. The observations support the idea that the can is made of steel, but do not prove it; other metals may have similar heat capacities. A list of the heat capacities of various metals for comparison would be helpful, as would other kinds of evidence, such as the densities and chemical properties of the metals.
4. The specific heat of the can is close to that of steel, not tin. This suggests that the can is made of steel.

Forensics Lab: Evaluating Electrical Safety

Objective

After completing this activity, students will be able to
- determine the voltage differences across resistances in series.

Prep Time 20 minutes

Advance Preparation

Strip insulation from the ends of the wires attached to the battery clips. Label the resistors with their resistances. Each resistor has four colored bands at one end. From the end of the resistor inward, the first three bands for the resistors used in this lab are 1 ohm: brown, black, gold; 10 ohms: brown, black, black; 100 ohms: brown, black, brown; and 1000 ohms: brown, black, red. The fourth band indicates the accuracy of the labeled resistance.

Class Time 45 minutes

Safety

Caution students to be careful with the sharp tips of the wires when assembling the circuit, and when handling the circuits that are turned on. The circuit parts may become hot.

Expected Outcome

The voltage difference across each resistor in the circuit is proportional to its resistance. The total voltage difference across both resistors is equal to the voltage of the battery, which may decline after the battery has been used.

Analyze and Conclude

1. The ratio of the voltage differences was 0.01 (1 : 100).
2. The voltage difference across each resistor was proportional to its resistance.
3. The resistance of the insulation should be 100 times the resistance of the current-carrying part.

Application Lab: Investigating an Electric Generator

Objective

After completing this activity, students will be able to
- describe how an electric generator works.

Prep Time 15 minutes

Sample Data

Current-Carrying Resistance (ohms)	Insulating Resistance (ohms)	Current-Carrying Voltage Difference (volts)	Insulating Voltage Difference (volts)
1	1000	0.01	9.0
1	100	0.09	7.6
10	1000	0.09	8.9
10	100	0.82	7.9

Advance Prep

Cut a 5-m length of wire for each group and strip 3 cm of the insulation from the ends of the wires. Provide cardboard tubes from empty bathroom paper rolls.

Class Time 45 minutes

Safety

Students should wear safety goggles and lab aprons.

Teaching Tips

- In Step 16 and subsequent steps, make sure that students read the sign or direction of the current correctly. In Step 16, this information will be the reverse of the direction observed in the previous steps.
- Show students how to insert the bar magnet so that the center of the bar is in line with the coils. The magnet should always be released at the same point.
- When dropping the bar magnet through the coil, students should place something soft on the floor below to avoid damaging or disturbing the magnetic field of the magnets.

Expected Outcome

The current is directly proportional to the number of coils. Reversing the poles of the magnet or the direction of the coils reverses the direction of the current.

Answers to Analyze and Conclude

1. A current flowed in the wire because the moving magnetic field exerted a force on the electrons in the wire, causing them to move.
2. The graph indicates a direct proportion between the number of coils and the current.
3. Reversing the direction of the magnet or the coils reversed the direction of the force of the magnetic field on the electrons in the wire. This change in direction caused the current to flow in the opposite direction.
4. It does not matter which part moves to accomplish this task. It is only necessary that the magnetic field in the wire coil change.
5. A correct prediction should state that reversing the direction of the magnet or the wire coils will reverse the direction of the current.

Sample Data

Number of Coils	Direction of Coils	Pole Inserted	Current (mA)
10	Clockwise	North	0.0136
20	Clockwise	North	0.0268
30	Clockwise	North	0.0430
30	Counterclockwise	South	−0.0411
30	Clockwise	North	−0.0391

Exploration Lab: Determining Relative Humidity

Objective
After completing this activity, students will be able to
- explain how to determine relative humidity.

Address Misconceptions
Students may confuse relative humidity and absolute humidity. Explain that relative humidity is not an absolute measurement of the amount of moisture in the atmosphere. Point out to students that relative humidity is expressed as a percentage of the maximum possible absolute humidity at a particular temperature. A common misconception is that relative humidity is a percentage of the water-holding capacity of air. Unlike liquid solvents that have a finite ability to dissolve various solids, air does not have a temperature-dependent holding capacity for water vapor. Rather, 100% relative humidity describes a situation in which the water vapor in the air is in equilibrium with the vapor pressure above a surface of pure water. Many people believe incorrectly that humid air is denser than dry air. Use a periodic table to show students that the water molecule's molecular mass is substantially less than those of N_2 and O_2 that account for nearly all the mass of dry air.

Prep Time 15 minutes

Advance Prep
Make certain that the relative humidity charts that you supply to students express temperatures in degrees Celsius, to match the temperature probe measurements that students will use in the lab.

Class Time 40 minutes

Teaching Tips
- When recording measurements outside of the classroom, be sure that your interface box has fresh batteries.
- Designate a second location at which to record the relative humidity in Step 6. This site could be outdoors, the cafeteria, or a hallway.

Expected Outcome
The wet-bulb temperature probe will have a lower temperature than the dry-bulb temperature probe.

Sample Data
Typical data could consist of a dry-bulb reading of 21°C, a wet-bulb reading of 15°C, and a relative humidity of 51%. Data will depend on local conditions. In any case, the wet-bulb reading will be less than or equal to the dry-bulb reading.

Analyze and Conclude
1. The temperature of the wet-bulb temperature probe is usually lower than the temperature of the dry-bulb temperature probe because evaporation of water from the wet bulb absorbed energy from the wet-bulb temperature probe, which cooled the temperature probe.
2. The difference in temperature between the two temperature probes depends on the degree to which evaporation cools the wet bulb. The lower the relative humidity, the greater is the rate at which water evaporates, cooling the wet bulb. Relative humidity does not affect the temperature of the dry-bulb temperature probe. Therefore, the lower the relative humidity, the cooler the wet bulb will be, and the greater the difference in temperature between the two temperature probes will be.
3. Factors that are likely to affect the relative humidity in various locations include sources of water, especially warm water, and variation in the effectiveness of heating and cooling throughout the school building.
4. Cooling the room would increase the relative humidity. The maximum concentration of water vapor in air is reduced at lower temperatures. Therefore, as the air in the room is cooled, the same concentration of water vapor becomes a higher percentage of the maximum concentration, or a higher relative humidity.

Go Further
Relative humidity is typically highest in early morning due to evaporation of moisture condensed during the night. Students may observe additional patterns of change in relative humidity depending on location, current weather conditions, and the season.